Similarity Joins in
Relational Database Systems

Synthesis Lectures on Data Management

Editor
M. Tamer Özsu, *University of Waterloo*

Synthesis Lectures on Data Management is edited by Tamer Özsu of the University of Waterloo. The series publishes 50- to 125 page publications on topics pertaining to data management. The scope will largely follow the purview of premier information and computer science conferences, such as ACM SIGMOD, VLDB, ICDE, PODS, ICDT, and ACM KDD. Potential topics include, but not are limited to: query languages, database system architectures, transaction management, data warehousing, XML and databases, data stream systems, wide scale data distribution, multimedia data management, data mining, and related subjects.

Similarity Joins in Relational Database Systems
Nikolaus Augsten and Michael H. Böhlen
2013

Data Cleaning: A Practical Perspective
Venkatesh Ganti and Anish Das Sarma
2013

Data Processing on FPGAs
Jens Teubner and Louis Woods
2013

Perspectives on Business Intelligence
Raymond T. Ng, Patricia C. Arocena, Denilson Barbosa, Giuseppe Carenini, Luiz Gomes, Jr. Stephan Jou, Rock Anthony Leung, Evangelos Milios, Renée J. Miller, John Mylopoulos, Rachel A. Pottinger, Frank Tompa, and Eric Yu
2013

Semantics Empowered Web 3.0: Managing Enterprise, Social, Sensor, and Cloud-based Data and Services for Advanced Applications
Amit Sheth and Krishnaprasad Thirunarayan
2012

Data Management in the Cloud: Challenges and Opportunities
Divyakant Agrawal, Sudipto Das, and Amr El Abbadi
2012

Similarity Joins in Relational Database Systems
Nikolaus Augsten and Michael H. Böhlen

ISBN: 978-3-031-00723-1   paperback
ISBN: 978-3-031-01851-0   ebook

DOI 10.2200/978-3-031-01851-0

A Publication in the Springer series
SYNTHESIS LECTURES ON DATA MANAGEMENT

Lecture #38
Series Editor: M. Tamer Özsu, *University of Waterloo*
Series ISSN
Synthesis Lectures on Data Management
Print 2153-5418   Electronic 2153-5426

Similarity Joins in Relational Database Systems

Nikolaus Augsten
University of Salzburg

Michael H. Böhlen
University of Zürich

SYNTHESIS LECTURES ON DATA MANAGEMENT #38

ABSTRACT

State-of-the-art database systems manage and process a variety of complex objects, including strings and trees. For such objects equality comparisons are often not meaningful and must be replaced by similarity comparisons. This book describes the concepts and techniques to incorporate similarity into database systems. We start out by discussing the properties of strings and trees, and identify the edit distance as the de facto standard for comparing complex objects. Since the edit distance is computationally expensive, token-based distances have been introduced to speed up edit distance computations. The basic idea is to decompose complex objects into sets of tokens that can be compared efficiently. Token-based distances are used to compute an approximation of the edit distance and prune expensive edit distance calculations.

A key observation when computing similarity joins is that many of the object pairs, for which the similarity is computed, are very different from each other. Filters exploit this property to improve the performance of similarity joins. A filter preprocesses the input data sets and produces a set of candidate pairs. The distance function is evaluated on the candidate pairs only. We describe the essential query processing techniques for filters based on lower and upper bounds. For token equality joins we describe prefix, size, positional and partitioning filters, which can be used to avoid the computation of small intersections that are not needed since the similarity would be too low.

KEYWORDS

strings, trees, similarity, edit distance, q-grams, pq-grams, token-based distance, lower bound, upper bound, similarity join

To Leni, Magdalena, and Katharina.
Nikolaus

To Franziska, Chantal, and Pascal.
Michael

Contents

6.2.1 Prefix Filter for Overlap Similarity 83

6.2.2 Prefix Filter for Jaccard Similarity 85

6.2.3 Effectiveness of Prefix Filtering 86

6.3 Size Filter 87

6.4 Positional Filter 87

6.5 Partitioning Filter 88

6.6 Further Readings 88

7 **Conclusion** **91**

Bibliography **93**

Authors' Biographies **103**

Index **105**

Preface

During the last few decades database systems have evolved substantially and today it is common for database systems to manage a large variety of complex objects. At the physical level, there has been significant progress in terms of storing and processing such complex objects. At the logical level, however, complex objects remain a challenge. A key reason is that equality, which is appropriate for simple objects, is often ineffective for complex objects. In this book we describe the essential concepts and techniques toward a principled solution for processing complex objects that must be compared in terms of similarity rather than equality.

An intuitive approach to define the similarity of complex objects is the edit distance, i.e., the number of basic edit operations that are required to transform one object into another. The intuitive nature of the edit distance is the reason why edit distances have become the de facto standard for complex objects. We define the string and tree edit distance, give algorithms to compute these distances, and work out the essential properties that support the effective and efficient processing of complex objects.

Token distances, which decompose complex objects into sets of tokens, have been proposed to deal with the high computational cost of edit distances. The token distance is computed by comparing the token sets that are the result of the decompositions. The more similar two token sets are the smaller is their distance. Token sets are compared by counting the number of identical elements in the sets. Set intersection is an operation that is well supported by database systems and scales to large sets. We survey the different techniques to compute and process token sets, and we discuss in detail three representative decomposition techniques: strings with q-grams, ordered trees with pq-grams, and unordered trees with windowed pq-grams.

Determining the exact distance between complex objects, particularly for joins where all pairs of objects must be compared, is often too expensive. To reduce the costs of such computations, filter and refine approaches have been developed. The goal of the filter step is to cheaply identify candidate pairs for which the exact similarity must be computed. Non-candidate pairs do not have to be considered because their similarity is not sufficient to be included in the result. We describe various filter techniques, and provide lower and upper bounds that can be used to efficiently compute similarity joins.

The book uses strings and trees as representative examples of complex objects. The techniques discussed in this book, however, are general and are also applicable to other types of objects. In particular, graphs are an important data structure that recently have received a lot of attention, and for which edit- and token-based distances have been proposed. At the relevant places we provide references to the vibrant and emerging field of graphs in databases.

The book is intended as a starting point for researchers and students in the database field who would like to learn more about similarity in database systems. Throughout, we offer precisely defined concepts and properties, and we illustrate these with representative and carefully chosen examples. We made an effort to include precise definitions, theorems, and examples, but at the same time kept the description at a level that is understandable to a general audience with an academic background. Much of the material presented in this book has been used in courses taught during the last few years at the Free University of Bozen-Bolzano, Technische Universität München, University of Salzburg, and University of Zürich. Our warm thanks goes to the students who provided constructive feedback and helped to advance the material presented in this book.

Nikolaus Augsten and Michael H. Böhlen
October 2013

Acknowledgments

Several people offered valuable support during the preparation of this book. We warmly thank Tamer Özsu for inviting us to write this lecture, and we thank Diane Cerra for her perfect management of the entire process. We thank both Tamer and Diane for their kind but firm pushes that helped us to make this lecture happen.

Part of the book's material evolved from courses and lectures taught at the Free University of Bozen-Bolzano, Technische Universität München, the University of Salzburg, and the University of Zürich. We thank the many students for their constructive comments and their patience with early versions of the course material.

Tatsuya Akutsu and Robert Elsässer contributed with feedback about the unordered tree edit distance and its complexity, Willi Mann helped with proofreading the book. We would also like to acknowledge the many collaborators and friends who, through discussions and comments have shaped our thinking and understanding of the area: Arturas Mazeika, Chen Li, Johann Gamper, Denilson Barbosa, Themis Palpanas, Curtis Dyreson, Mateusz Pawlik, Jan Finis, Martin Raiber, Theo Härder, Leonardo Andrade Ribeiro, Benjamin Gufler, Gerard Lemson, Walter Costanzi, Franco Barducci, and Roberto Loperfido.

Finally, we would like to acknowledge our funding sources: Michael Böhlen's work is supported by the University of Zürich, the Swiss National Science Foundation, and the Free University of Bozen-Bolzano. Nikolaus Augsten's work is supported by the University of Salzburg, the Free University of Bozen-Bolzano, the Department for Promotion of Educational Policies, University and Research of the Autonomous Province of Bolzano - South Tyrol, and Technische Universität München.

Nikolaus Augsten and Michael H. Böhlen
October 2013

CHAPTER 1

Introduction

Many applications rely on database systems for storing and querying data. Most often these are extensions of relational database systems, which build on strong theoretical foundations and mature technology that has been developed and advanced for decades. Current database systems focus on *exact* queries to, e.g., look up customers by their social security number, compute average sales per department, or join tables on keys and foreign keys. Unfortunately, for complex data types likes strings or trees, such queries often lead to poor results since two data items may be different even if they represent the same real world object.

In the case of strings, differences may happen due to typos, varying coding conventions used by different users or companies (e.g., `Transactions on Database Systems` versus `Trans. on Database Systems`), errors introduced by the OCR software, poor quality entries from information retrieval software, etc.

In the case of trees, which store the hierarchical relationship between individual data items, content as well as structure may differ. A popular example is XML, which organizes data items in a tree structure. Data sources that store information about the same object may represent it differently. For example, both DBLP and SIGMOD Record store bibliographic data about scientific articles in XML, but they use different structures to represent them. Even if the structure of two XML sources is the same, one of the sources may store more information than the other source, for example, in optional elements and attributes. Although there is no exact match between the XML fragments that represent the same scientific article, their XML trees are likely to be more similar than the XML fragments of different articles.

1.1 APPLICATIONS OF SIMILARITY QUERIES

Joining XML about Music Albums   As an application example consider an online database about music CDs that integrates data from two XML sources: a song lyric store and a CD warehouse. The integrated database will store the artists and songs of an album, information about individual songs such as the lyrics, guitar tabs, and information about the artists.

Figure 1.1 shows tree representations of two different XML documents. Both represent data about the same song album. Yet exact, ordered tree matching would not consider the items as the same for a number of reasons. The song lyric store has an element `year` that is absent from the CD warehouse. The CD warehouse has a price for the album. For one track the databases list different artists. Also the document order of elements differs, i.e., the two documents have different sibling orders.

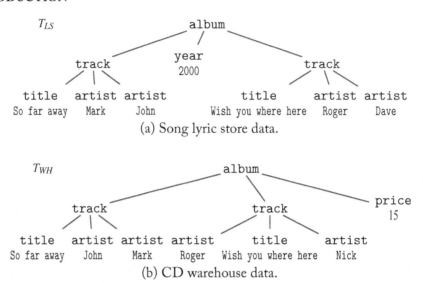

(a) Song lyric store data.

(b) CD warehouse data.

Figure 1.1: Two XML trees representing the same album.

In order to match two XML fragments about the same album, a similarity measure between trees is required. Since the order in which the elements are stored should not matter, a tree similarity measure for this application should consider two trees to be similar even if the order of the elements is different.

Street Matching   In some applications the tree structure is not explicit (like in XML), but is implicit in the data. Consider Figure 1.2, which shows two example tables with street names and addresses. Both tables in Figure 1.2 store residential addresses that cover the same geographical region. The Ownr table stores the owner and the Rsdt table the resident of each property. A query that retrieves owner and residents for each apartment must join the tables on the residential addresses.

Clearly, matching streets from Ownr and Rsdt is non-trivial and an exact join returns an empty result set. For example, Cimitero and Friedhofsplatz, Via Bivio and Kaiserau, and Friedensplatz and Siegesplatz are matching pairs of streets. In all cases string comparison performs poorly. Besides streets that match, there are also streets with similar names that are indeed different and may not be matched. For example, Trienterstr and Triesterstr are different streets as are Rentscherstr and Reschenstr. In both cases, the street names are similar and a string comparison might wrongly match these street pairs.

To reliably match streets it is necessary to exploit the information about the structure of streets. Toward this end the addresses of single streets can be organized hierarchically and represented as *address trees* [Augsten et al., 2004]. Figure 1.3 shows the address trees for streets Via Bivio and Kaiserau in Figure 1.2. The root of the tree is the street name, the children of the

Ownr					Rsdt				
s1	n1	e1	a1	owner	s2	n2	e2	a2	resident
Cimitero	4	–	–	Rose	Friedhofplatz	4	–	–	Dario
Cimitero	6	–	–	Lara	Friedhofplatz	6	A	–	Luigi
Friedensplatz	2	A	1	Igor	Friedhofplatz	6	B	–	Marc
Friedensplatz	2	A	2	Sarah	Kaiserau	1	–	1	Peter
Friedensplatz	3	–	–	Sue	Kaiserau	1	–	2	Lena
Mariengasse	1	A	–	Linas	Kaiserau	1	–	3	Lena
Rentscherstr	1	–	–	Pia	Kaiserau	2	A	–	Anita
Rentscherstr	2	–	–	Tony	Mariengasse	1	–	–	Adam
Trienterstr	1	A	1	Tom	Reschenstr	1	A	1	Tony
Trienterstr	1	A	2	Tom	Triesterstr	1	–	–	Ron
Trienterstr	1	A	3	Pam	Siegesplatz	2	A	1	Martin
Via Bivio	1	–	1	Peter	Siegesplatz	3	–	1	Leo
Via Bivio	1	–	3	John	Siegesplatz	3	–	2	Maria
Via Bivio	2	A	–	Marc	Siegesplatz	3	–	3	Rosa
...					...				

Figure 1.2: Tables with owner (Ownr) and resident (Rsdt) information.

street name are the house numbers, the children of house numbers are the entrance numbers, and the children of entrance numbers are the apartment numbers. We omit empty values ("–") in the leaves of address trees. A complete address is the path from the root to any leaf node. For example, the tuple (Via Bivio, 2, A, –) of table Ownr represents the address Via Bivio 2A and corresponds to the shaded path in Figure 1.3.

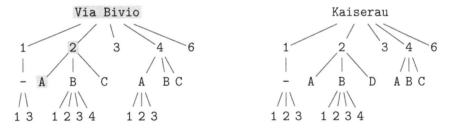

Figure 1.3: Address trees of streets Via Bivio from Ownr and Kaiserau from Rsdt.

Intuitively, two streets match if they have similar address trees. To improve the quality of the street matches not only the string similarity between street names should be considered but also the structure of their address trees.

Merger Trees of Galaxies   So far we have considered applications in which two data items should be matched if they represent the same object in the real world. Another class of applications looks for distinct but similar objects. This query pattern is frequent in natural sciences where, e.g., biologists search for similar carbohydrate molecules [Aoki et al., 2003] or similarities in RNA secondary structures [Blin et al., 2010].

Another example are so-called *merger trees*, which are used in astrophysics to model the evolution of galaxies over time. The leaf nodes in a merger tree are galaxies distributed in the universe at an early point in time. Due to the interaction between masses, the galaxies merge and form new galaxies. The event of two (or more) merging galaxies is modeled as an inner node in the merger tree. The root node of a merger tree represents the galaxy that results from the various merging steps. Astrophysicists are interested in the relation between the properties of galaxies and the shapes of their merger trees (i.e., the evolutionary history of a galaxy).

Merger trees are amongst the most important methods for studying the growth and development of galaxies and dark matter halos in numerical simulations. A well known simulation of this type is the Millennium Simulation [Springel et al., 2005], which produced 25 TB of raw output data, forming over 18.5 million trees with a total of approximately 760 million nodes. Finding subsets of similar trees in such a large set of trees requires efficient similarity measures. Different from XML or address trees, the nodes are not labeled with strings that can be compared for equality. Instead, the nodes store numerical data about the galaxies that they represent, for example, mass, position, redshift, and spin.

1.2   EDIT-BASED SIMILARITY MEASURES

In order to answer similarity queries, the similarity between data items must be computed. Various similarity measures for strings and trees have been proposed. An interesting class of similarity measures are edit-based similarities.

Edit-based similarity measures express the difference between two objects by the number of basic edit operations that are required to transform one object into the other. The smaller the number of required edit operations, the more similar the objects are. For string data, for example, the canonical set of edit operations is a) deleting a character, b) inserting a character, and c) replacing a character. With this set of edit operations, two edit operations are required to transform `police` into `olive` (deleting p and replacing c by v). Since the similarity decreases with the number of edit operations, the alikeness of two objects is often expressed as a dissimilarity rather than a similarity, i.e., as a distance. In our example the distance between `police` and `olive` is two.

Edit-based distances enjoy some features that made them very popular across a large number of applications.

- The definition of edit-based distances is very *intuitive* and easy to understand.

- The distance guarantees the *minimal* sequence of edit operations, setting it apart from many distance measures that cannot provide any guarantees.

- In addition to a numeric distance value, also the corresponding edits (called *edit script*) can be computed, which is useful, for example, for versioning tools.

• Edit distances allow very *flexible cost models* and can thus be tailored to different applications without a change in the algorithm.

The main challenge with edit-based distances is their high computational complexity. The edit distance for strings (with insertion, deletion, and replacement), for example, requires quadratic runtime and linear space in the length of the string. This may be acceptable for short strings like customer names, but it is a serious limitation for long strings like RNA primary structures. In database systems, the use of edit-based distances is challenging also for short strings due to the many distance computations that are required in typical queries.

1.3   TOKEN-BASED SIMILARITY MEASURES

Among the most common and important similarity queries in a database are similarity joins (pairing tuples from two different tables if a similarity predicate is satisfied), similarity grouping (grouping a single table into groups of similar tuples, for example, for duplicate elimination), and ranking (the k tuples that are most similar to the query tuple).

These queries rely on similarity predicates that are often expressed as a distance function together with a matching threshold. The predicate is satisfied for two objects if the distance between them is within the threshold. Distance functions can be implemented as user-defined functions (UDFs), and database systems typically allow UDFs be written in various languages like C/C++, Java, or Visual Basic.

Evaluating a join based on a similarity predicate requires the evaluation of the predicate for each pair of tuples, leading to a quadratic number of calls to the UDF. Even if the runtime for a single call to the UDF is short, i.e., the similarity function can be evaluated efficiently, this approach does not scale with the size of the joined tables. For example, if the predicate is evaluated in $0.01ms$, joining two tables with 1k tuples each takes 10 seconds, while joining two tables with 100k tuples each will take 27 hours.

Edit-based distances are usually implemented as main memory dynamic programming algorithms and their evaluation is a black box to the database systems. New techniques that are closer to the concept of tuples and relations used in databases are required. Queries that are expressed over relations and use relational operators can be optimized and evaluated efficiently by the database system.

A frequent approach for similarity queries are filters. A filter discards unpromising tuples before the similarity predicate is evaluated. The evaluation of the filter is much faster than the evaluation of the similarity predicate, thus leading to an overall improved runtime. Good filters produce no false negatives, i.e., all tuples discarded by the filter are in fact non-matches. Thus, the runtime is improved without sacrificing the quality of matches.

Various filters have been proposed for edit-based distances. Our main focus are token-based filters. Tokens are snippets of the objects that should be compared. Examples of tokens are the words of a document, substrings of fixed length of a string (called q-grams), or subtrees of a fixed shape of a tree (called pq-grams). Tokens are used to assess the similarity of two objects.

Intuitively, two objects are similar if they share many tokens. For example, two text documents are considered similar if they have many words in common.

Token-based filters represent objects by sets (or multisets) of tokens and express the similarity between objects using set operations like intersection. This makes token-based filters very appealing for relational database systems, which are geared to sets and multisets. Token-based filters have been developed for many data types, including strings [Li et al., 2007, Ukkonen, 1992], trees [Augsten et al., 2005], and graphs [Zhao et al., 2012].

Tokens are not only used as filters, but also as similarity measures on their own. Token-based similarity measures are typically much more efficient than edit-based similarities and they scale to large objects. For example, the pq-gram distance between trees requires $O(n \log n)$ time and $O(n)$ space for trees with n nodes, whereas the tree edit distance requires $O(n^3)$ time and $O(n^2)$ space. Further, a number of techniques have been developed that can avoid the pairwise comparison of objects in similarity joins with tokens. Using these techniques, token-based similarity joins are transformed to equality joins on tokens, which are evaluated efficiently using well-known join algorithms like hash join or sort-merge join.

In this book we survey edit-based distances and token-based distances for string and trees. We discuss algorithms to compute pairwise distances and join techniques using token-based filters.

CHAPTER 2

Data Types

2.1 STRINGS

Strings are among the most important primitive data types in information systems. They appear, for example, as text documents, as text values in XML data, or as attributes of relational tables. Due to the many inconsistencies found in string data, for example because of spelling mistakes or different representations, similarity queries over string data have received much attention in the literature. String similarity queries are also used in bioinformatics to match the primary structure of RNA sequences, which are encoded as strings over a four-character alphabet. In this context, similarity must deal with mutations and find similar regions in the RNA string.

Strings are sequences of characters. The similarity algorithms for strings presented hereafter also work for the general case of sequences. The only condition is that elements must be mutually comparable using equality.

Following the SQL standard, string types are supported in off-the-shelf database systems as CHAR (fixed length, blank padded) or VARCHAR (variable length) types; most systems also have an additional string type of arbitrary length, for example, TEXT in PostgreSQL.

2.2 TREES

Data items that are organized in hierarchies form trees. In tree data, part of the information is encoded in the parent-child relationships between the nodes in the tree. For example, in an organizational chart, the fact that Mary is stored in the parent node and John in the child node expresses the fact that Mary is John's boss. Examples of hierarchical data are HTML documents, XML data, file systems, parse trees in linguistics, melody trees in music information retrieval, carbohydrate molecules and RNA secondary structures in biology, or merger trees in astrophysics.

Structure of Trees   We define trees as directed, acyclic, connected graphs with at most one incoming edge per node. The root node has no incoming edge, and leaf nodes have no outgoing edges. Edges point from a parent to its children. The children of a node are strictly and totally ordered; the smallest node in the child order is called the leftmost (or first) child, the largest child is the rightmost child. The *fanout* of a node is the number of its children. The set of all nodes of a tree T is $N(T)$. We use the abbreviation $|T|$ for the number of tree nodes $|N(T)|$ and write $n \in T$ for $n \in N(T)$.

A *label* $\lambda(n)$ is assigned to each node n. Labels may be of any data type. When XML is modeled as trees, the label is typically a string. In the case of merger trees (cf. Section 1.1), the labels are relational tuples of numeric values. Some tree similarity measures assume an equality relation between labels. This is intuitive for string labels or categorical labels, but on the real-valued labels of merger trees equality is less meaningful.

Tree nodes are always uniquely identified in the tree, but multiple nodes can have identical labels. An example tree is shown in Figure 2.1, where the node identifiers are shown as subscript numbers. The nodes 5 and 9 (label b) and the nodes 2 and 3 (label c) have identical labels, respectively. In the graphical representation, the direction of the edges (from parent to child) is omitted.

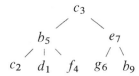

Figure 2.1: Example tree.

Ordered and Unordered Trees   Another important property of tree data is the relevance of the child order. For example, in music albums the order of the children does not matter since the order of the title and artist nodes of a track is not relevant. In HTML documents, the order of the paragraph nodes is highly relevant since reordering these nodes reorders the paragraphs in the text. The matching problem is typically harder when the order of the children must be ignored. For example, the edit distance for trees can be computed in polynomial time if the children order should matter, but the problem is NP-hard if the children order should not be taken into consideration [Zhang et al., 1992].

Trees in which the order of the children should not matter are often referred to as *unordered trees*. In our definition, trees are always ordered. If the order of the children should not matter for their similarity, *tree permutations* are used to model the non-relevance of the order. Ordered trees are *permutations* of each other if they differ only in the sibling order. In the unordered case, two trees are considered identical if one tree is the permutation of the other tree. A permutation of a tree T is denoted as $\pi(T)$, the set of all permutations of T as $\Pi(T)$. In a *sorted tree* the siblings are lexicographically ordered by their node labels.

Example 2.1   Figure 2.2 shows an ordered tree T together with two different permutations, $\pi_1(T)$ and $\pi_2(T)$. Permutation $\pi_2(T)$ is a sorted tree; since the root node has two children with label c, the sorting is not unique.

XML and Trees   In order to apply similarity queries to XML, we represent an XML document as a labeled tree.

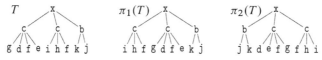

Figure 2.2: Permuted trees.

We distinguish document centric and data centric XML. An example of document centric XML is XHTML. In document centric XML the order of the children matters and an element can contain both text and sub-elements. Each node in the labeled tree represents an XML tag, an attribute name, the value of an attribute, or the text between two elements. An edge connects an element node with each of its sub-elements or attributes. We sort all attributes lexicographically by their name and place them before all element nodes in the tree. Consider the example XML fragment in Figure 2.3 and the corresponding tree. The first paragraph contains both text and a sub-element (`<em>...</em>`), the order of the nodes is relevant.

```
<body>
  <p>This is <em>document centric</em> XML.</p>
  <p>This is the second paragraph.</p>
</body>
```

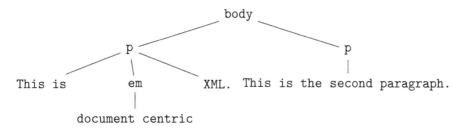

Figure 2.3: Document centric XML.

In data centric XML the order of the elements does not matter and elements have either sub-elements or a text value. In addition to the tree model presented for document centric XML, a second tree model can be used: A node in the tree represents an XML element (or attribute). The node label is a *(tag, value)* pair, where *tag* is the name of the element (or attribute) and *value* is the text content of the corresponding element (or attribute). If the corresponding element contains only sub-elements and no content, then the node value is the empty string, ϵ. An edge connects an element node with each of its sub-elements (or attributes). An example is shown in Figure 2.4.

```
<article type="journal" key="codd70">
  <author>Codd</author>
  <title>Relational Model</title>
  <year>1970</year>
</article>
```

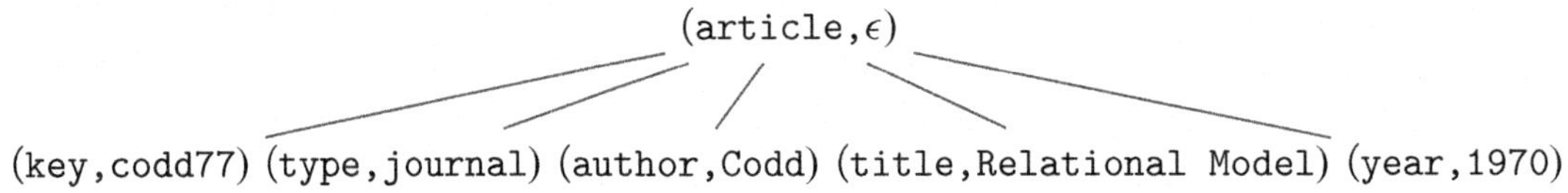

$$(\texttt{article},\epsilon)$$

$(\texttt{key},\texttt{codd77})$ $(\texttt{type},\texttt{journal})$ $(\texttt{author},\texttt{Codd})$ $(\texttt{title},\texttt{Relational Model})$ $(\texttt{year},\texttt{1970})$

Figure 2.4: Data centric XML.

CHAPTER 3

Edit-Based Distances

3.1 STRING EDIT DISTANCE

3.1.1 DEFINITION OF THE STRING EDIT DISTANCE

The *edit distance* between two strings is the minimum number of edit operations that transform one string into another. Allowable edit operations are the insertion of a new character, deletion of a character, and replacing a character in the string by another character. The edit distance was introduced by Levenshtein [1965] for signal processing and is also known as *Levenshtein distance*.

Instead of counting the edit operations, a cost can be assigned to each operation. We introduce the empty character ϵ and denote the cost of transforming character a to character b by $c(a, b)$. The cost for inserting b is $c(\epsilon, b)$, the cost for deleting a is $c(a, \epsilon)$, the cost for replacing a by b, $a \neq \epsilon$, $b \neq \epsilon$ is $c(a, b)$; $c(a, b) = 0$ if $a = b$. In the *unit cost model* all costs $c(a, b)$, $a \neq b$, are one.

Definition 3.1 String Edit Distance. Let s_1 and s_2 be strings. The *string edit distance*, $\text{sed}(s_1, s_2)$, between s_1 and s_2 is the minimum cost sequence of node edit operations (insert a character, delete a character, replace a character) that transforms s_1 to s_2.

Example 3.2 Assuming the unit cost model, the edit distance between the strings $s_1 = \text{banana}$ and $s_2 = \text{ananas}$ is 2: remove the first character (b) from s_1 and insert a new character (s) at the end.

Metric Properties The string edit distance satisfies the metric properties if the cost function satisfies these properties, i.e., given characters a, b, d (which may also be the empty character) the following holds:

- $c(a, b) = 0 \Leftrightarrow a = b$ (identity)

- $c(a, b) = c(b, a)$ (symmetry)

- $c(a, d) + c(d, b) \geq c(a, b)$ (triangle inequality)

The unit cost model ($c(a, \epsilon) = c(\epsilon, b) = 1$, $c(a, b) = 1$ if $a \neq b$, $c(a, b) = 0$ if $a = b$) satisfies the metric properties and makes the unit cost edit distance a metric.

Normalization   The edit distance counts the differences between strings, but does not take into account the string length. This can lead to undesired effects. Consider, for example, the string pairs and their distances in Figure 3.1. The distance between IBM and BMW, which are the abbreviations for two different companies, is the same as the distance between International Business Machines Corporation and its misspelled variant. The strings International Business Machines Corporation and Int. Business Machines Corp., which obviously refer to the same company, are at a much larger distance than IBM and BMW.

sed(International Business Machines Corporation,
    International Bussiness Machine_Corporation) = 2
sed(IBM, BMW) = 2
sed(Int. Business Machines Corp.,
    International Business Machines Corporation) = 17

Figure 3.1: Non-normalized string edit distance.

For the string pairs in Figure 3.1 we cannot find a single distance threshold that distinguishes matches from non-matches. If we set the threshold to 17, such that all good pairs match, then also IBM and BMW will match. Note that for the threshold 17 any pair of strings with 17 or less characters will be classified as a match.

The value of the edit distance ranges between zero and the length of the longer string. We normalize the distance between two strings s_1 and s_2 (with length $|s_1|$ and $|s_2|$, respectively) to values between zero and one as follows:

$$sed_{norm}(s_1, s_2) = \frac{sed(s_1, s_2)}{\max(|s_1|, |s_2|)}$$

This distance is called the *normalized string edit distance*. Intuitively, it is the percentage of characters that need to be changed to turn one string into the other. The normalized edit distance is zero if and only if the two strings are identical; the maximum value for very different strings is 1.

Figure 3.2 shows the distance between the strings in the previous example. For the normalized edit distance we can find a threshold that distinguishes matches from non-matches, for example, the threshold 0.4.

Overall, the non-normalized edit distance is useful only for very small thresholds (e.g., when we allow a single typo) or when all involved strings are of similar length.

In some application scenarios even normalization does not help. For example, in the street matching scenario, the streets named Trienterstr and Triesterstr differ by only one character but are different streets. Another limitation of the edit distance are word transpositions. For example, the strings James Wood and Wood James refer to the same person, but are at distance 10, which is the maximum for two strings of length 10. Normalization does not help here: the normalized edit distance is 1.0.

sed$_{norm}$(International Business Machines Corporation,
        International Bussiness Machine_Corporation) $= 0.047$
sed$_{norm}$(IBM, BMW) $= 0.66$
sed$_{norm}$(Int. Business Machines Corp.,
        International Business Machines Corporation) $= 0.4$

Figure 3.2: Normalized string edit distance.

3.1.2   COMPUTATION OF THE STRING EDIT DISTANCE

The edit distance between two strings can be expressed recursively. We denote the i-th character of a string s_1 with $s_1[i]$ and the substring of the first i characters of s_1 with $s_1[1\ldots i]$ ($s_1[1\ldots 0]$ is the empty string ϵ). Then the edit distance between two strings s_1 and s_2 is

$$
\begin{aligned}
\mathrm{sed}(\epsilon, \epsilon) &= 0 \\
\mathrm{sed}(s_1[1..i], \epsilon) &= \mathrm{sed}(s_1[1..i-1], \epsilon) + c_{del} \\
\mathrm{sed}(\epsilon, s_2[1..j]) &= \mathrm{sed}(\epsilon, s_2[1..j-1]) + c_{ins} \\
\mathrm{sed}(s_1[1..i], s_2[1..j]) &= \min(\mathrm{sed}(s_1[1..i-1], s_2[1..j-1]) + c_{rep}, \\
&\qquad\quad \mathrm{sed}(s_1[1..i-1], s_2[1..j]) + c_{del}, \\
&\qquad\quad \mathrm{sed}(s_1[1..i], s_2[1..j-1]) + c_{ins})
\end{aligned}
$$

where $c_{del} = c(s_1[i], \epsilon)$ is the cost of deleting $s_1[i]$, $c_{ins} = c(\epsilon, s_2[j])$ is the cost of inserting $s_2[j]$, and $c_{rep} = c(s_1[i], s_2[j])$ is the cost of replacing $s_1[i]$ by $s_2[j]$; $c_{rep} = 0$ if $s_1[i] = s_2[j]$. The recursion removes the last character from s_1, from s_2, or from both s_1 and s_2. Given the distances between these substrings, the distance between s_1 and s_2 is the minimum of the distances between the substrings plus the cost of the operation that changes the last character.

A straightforward recursive implementation of the algorithm has exponential runtime since many subproblems are computed repeatedly. Fortunately there is a faster solution. A string s_1 of length n has only $n + 1$ (including the empty string) substrings of the form $s_1[1..i]$, $0 \leq i \leq n$. Since all subproblems are pairs of such substrings, the number of *different* subproblems is only quadratic in the length of the two strings. This is leveraged by a dynamic programming algorithm that fills a matrix of size $(n + 1) \times (m + 1)$ for two strings of length n and m, respectively.

Figure 3.3(a) shows the cost matrix that is filled by the dynamic programming algorithm for two strings $s_1 = $ ab and $s_2 = $ cb. An entry (i, j) of the cost matrix stores the distance between $s_1[1..i]$ and $s_2[1..j]$. The entry $(0, 0)$ is initialized with the distance 0 between two empty strings, the other fields are filled column by column using the recursive formula. The distance between s_1 and s_2 is stored in the lower right corner of the cost matrix. Figure 3.3(b) shows the recursion tree of all subproblems. Clearly, many subproblems are repeated in the recursion.

The runtime of the dynamic programming algorithm is $O(nm)$ for two strings of length n and m, respectively. The space complexity is $O(n)$ if n is the length of the shorter string. Linear

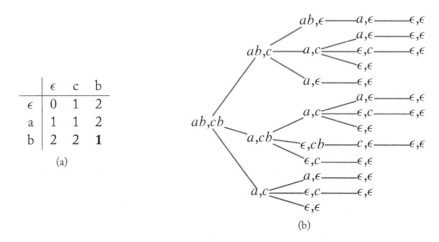

	ϵ	c	b
ϵ	0	1	2
a	1	1	2
b	2	2	1

(a)

(b)

Figure 3.3: Cost matrix for dynamic programming algorithm and full recursion tree.

space complexity is achieved by keeping only the current column col_1 and the previous column col_0 in main memory (see Algorithm 1). Older columns can be discarded.

Algorithm 1: StringEditDistance(s_1, s_2)

1 $col_0, col_1 : array[0..|s_1|]$;
2 $col_0[0] \leftarrow 0$;
3 **for** $i \leftarrow 1$ **to** $|s_1|$ **do** $col_0[i] \leftarrow col_0[i-1] + c_{del}$;
4 **for** $j \leftarrow 1$ **to** $|s_2|$ **do**
5 $\quad$ $col_1[0] \leftarrow col_0[0] + c_{ins}$;
6 $\quad$ **for** $i \leftarrow 1$ **to** $|s_1|$ **do**
7 $\quad\quad$ **if** $s_1[i] = s_2[j]$ **then** $c \leftarrow 0$;
8 $\quad\quad$ **else** $c \leftarrow c_{rep}$;
9 $\quad\quad$ $col_1[i] \leftarrow \min(col_0[i-1] + c, col_1[i-1] + c_{del}, col_0[i] + c_{ins})$;
10 $\quad$ $col_0 \leftarrow col_1$;

All minimal cost edit sequences can be derived from the cost matrix by walking through the matrix from the lower right corner to the upper left corner. In order to do this the old columns of the cost matrix cannot be discarded and the space complexity is $O(nm)$. Figure 3.4 illustrates the minimal edit sequences for transforming the string $s_1 = $ moon into $s_2 = $ mond. The scripts are the following:

- Solution 1: replace o (s_1[3]) by n; replace n by d

- Solution 2: delete o (s_1[2]); insert d after n

- Solution 3: delete o (s_1[3]); insert d after n

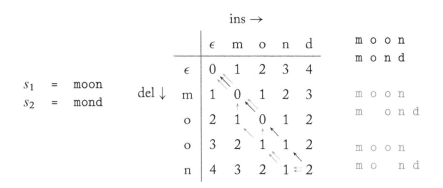

Figure 3.4: Edit script from cost matrix.

3.2 TREE EDIT DISTANCE

3.2.1 DEFINITION OF THE TREE EDIT DISTANCE

A well-known measure for comparing trees is the *tree edit distance*. Similar to the edit distance for strings, the edit distance for trees is defined as the minimum cost of a sequence of edit operations that transforms one tree into another, using the following three edit operations: *delete* a node and connect its children to its parent maintaining the sibling order (the root can only be deleted if it has a single child, which then becomes the root node); *insert* a new node between an existing node, p, and a subsequence of consecutive children of p; and *rename* the label of a node.

Example 3.3 Figure 3.5 illustrates the edit operations. T_1 is transformed into T_2 by inserting a new node x as the second child of the existing node a and substituting 3 children of a starting with child position 2. The substituted children become children of the new node x. Deleting node x transforms T_2 back to T_1. Renaming node a to z transforms T_2 into T_3.

Edit Mapping   An edit sequence between two trees produces a sequence of intermediate trees. Only the first operation in the sequence operates on the original tree. All other operations are defined on some intermediate tree. The intermediate trees depend on the order in which the nodes are deleted, inserted, and renamed. Considering the order of the edit operations adds complexity, but does not influence the cost of the edit sequence.

Figure 3.5: Tree edit operations.

An alternative definition of the tree edit distance ignores the order of the edit sequence and is based on so-called edit mappings. An edit mapping aligns the nodes of two trees following specific rules. Each node alignment has a cost. The tree edit distance is defined as the minimum cost edit mapping between two trees, where the cost of an edit mapping is the sum of costs of all alignments.

Let ϵ be the empty node and $N_\epsilon(T) = N(T) \cup \{\epsilon\}$ be the node set of tree T enriched with the empty node. A node v is *to the left* of a node w iff v precedes w in the preorder traversal of the tree and v is not an ancestor of w. The edit mapping is defined as follows: $M \subseteq N_\epsilon(T) \times N_\epsilon(T')$ is an *edit mapping between T and T'* iff

1. each node is mapped:

    (a) $\forall v[v \in T \Leftrightarrow \exists v'((v, v') \in M)]$

    (b) $\forall v'[v' \in T' \Leftrightarrow \exists v((v, v') \in M)]$

    (c) $(\epsilon, \epsilon) \notin M$

2. all pairs of non-empty nodes $(v, v'), (w, w') \in M$ satisfy the following conditions:

    (a) $v = w \Leftrightarrow v' = w'$ (one-to-one condition)

    (b) v is an ancestor of $w \Leftrightarrow v'$ is an ancestor of w' (ancestor condition)

    (c) v is to the left of $w \Leftrightarrow v'$ is to the left of w' (order condition)

A pair $(v, v') \in M$ is called a *node alignment*. Nodes of T that are mapped to the empty node are deleted, nodes of T' that are mapped to the empty node are inserted, and nodes that appear in mappings between non-empty nodes are renamed. A special case of rename is the rename with the identical label; these are the nodes that do not change between the trees.

A cost is assigned to each node alignment (i.e., to each edit operation). It depends on the involved nodes (the deleted node, the inserted node, or the two renamed nodes). The cost of the node alignment is zero if the labels of two mapped nodes are identical.

Metric Properties   The tree edit distance satisfies the metric properties (identity, symmetry, and triangle inequality) if the cost of the node alignments satisfies this property. More specifically, the cost $c(v, w)$ of aligning two (potentially empty) nodes v and w is zero if and only if v and w have the same label (identity), $c(v, w) = c(w, v)$ (symmetry), and $c(v, x) \leq c(v, w) + c(w, x)$ (triangle inequality).

Normalization   Similar to the edit distance for strings, also for the tree edit distance the normalization is useful to take into account the size of the compared trees. For the unit cost model, where all node alignments (i.e., all edit operations) have cost 1, the maximum edit distance between two trees is smaller than the sum of their numbers of nodes. The normalized tree edit distance

$$\text{ted}_{norm}(T, T') = \frac{\text{ted}(T, T')}{|T| + |T'|}$$

ranges between the values zero and one ($|T|$ denotes the number of nodes of tree T).

Fanout Weighted Tree Edit Distance   The unit cost model reduces the tree edit distance to the minimum number of edit operations that transforms one tree into the other. It does not distinguish between nodes with small and large fanout. This behavior leads to non-intuitive results, as illustrated in Figure 3.6. Tree T_1 is the result of deleting the leaves with labels g and k from T_2, whereas T_3 is obtained from T_2 by deleting the nodes labeled c and e. Intuitively, T_1 and T_2 are much more similar (in structure) than T_3 and T_2, but the unit cost tree edit distance ted_{unit} is 2 in both cases.

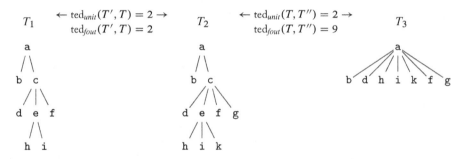

Figure 3.6: Tree edit distance with unit cost (ted_{unit}) and fanout weighted (ted_{fout}) cost model.

A cost model that takes into account the fanout of a node is the fanout weighting. The fanout weighted tree edit distance weighs leaf and non-leaf changes differently. The cost of an alignment is proportional to the fanout of the aligned nodes: Let T and T' be ordered labeled trees, let $k > 0$ be a constant, $v \in N_\epsilon(T)$, $v' \in N_\epsilon(T')$. The *cost of an alignment*, $c(v, v')$, is defined as $c(v, v') = 0$ if nodes v and v' have identical labels ($\lambda(v) = \lambda(v')$), otherwise:

$$c(v, v') = \begin{cases} f_v + k & \text{if } v \neq \epsilon \wedge v' = \epsilon \text{ (delete)} \\ f_{v'} + k & \text{if } v = \epsilon \wedge v' \neq \epsilon \text{ (insert)} \\ \frac{f_v + f_{v'}}{2} + k & \text{if } v \neq \epsilon \wedge v' \neq \epsilon \wedge \lambda(v) \neq \lambda(v') \text{ (rename)} \end{cases}$$

Thus, the cost of aligning leaf nodes is a constant k for all edit operations. For the other nodes the cost of deletion and insertion is proportional to the node's fanout. The choice of the rename cost should depend on the costs of deletion and insertion. The maximum meaningful cost of rename is below the cost of deletion plus insertion. If the rename cost is larger, then rename can always be substituted by deletion and insertion at lower cost, and rename is never used in the cheapest edit sequence. If the rename cost is small compared to the costs of insertion and deletion, then the cheapest edit sequence optimizes on aligning the structure and ignores the labels. A reasonable cost for rename is the average between the costs of deletion and insertion.

3.2.2   COMPUTATION OF THE TREE EDIT DISTANCE

Similar to the string edit distance, the tree edit distance can also be expressed in a recursive formula. The dynamic programming algorithms for the tree edit distance are more sophisticated, however. The difficulty comes from the number of subproblems. While a string of length n has only $O(n)$ substrings that can appear in the recursion, a tree with n nodes has $O(n^2)$ such subtrees. Thus, a straightforward memoization algorithm requires $O(n^4)$ space to store the distance result for all pairs of subtrees.

Zhang and Shasha [1989] developed the first dynamic programming algorithm that runs in $O(n^2)$ space. The algorithm saves space by overwriting results for subproblems when they are no longer needed. The algorithm of Zhang and Shasha requires $O(n^2 \min^2(l, h))$ time for trees with n nodes, l leaves, and height h; thus, for balanced trees with height $h = O(\log(n))$ the runtime is $O(n^2 \log^2(n))$. In the worst case, the algorithm requires $O(n^4)$ time. Much of the later work [Demaine et al., 2007, Dulucq and Touzet, 2003, Klein, 1998] strives to reduce the number of subproblems that need to be computed to reduce the runtime of the algorithm. The latest development is the RTED (Robust Tree Edit Distance) algorithm [Pawlik and Augsten, 2011]. RTED is guaranteed to compute the least number of subproblems for any instance among all dynamic programming algorithms. It runs in $O(n^2)$ space and has optimal $O(n^3)$ worst case complexity. Java implementations of the tree edit distance algorithms by Zhang and Shasha [1989], Klein [1998], Demaine et al. [2007], and Pawlik and Augsten [2011] are available online.[1]

3.2.3   CONSTRAINED TREE EDIT DISTANCE

Modifying the constraints on the edit mapping defines new distance functions. We describe the *constrained edit distance* [Guha et al., 2002, Zhang, 1995], which is used to speed up similarity joins (cf. Section 5.4.6).

A mapping $M_c \subseteq N_\epsilon(T) \times N_\epsilon(T')$ between the nodes of two trees T and T' is a *constrained edit mapping* iff M_c is an edit mapping (cf. Section 3.2.1) and all pairs of non-empty nodes (v, v'), (w, w'), $(x, x') \in M_c$ satisfy the additional fourth condition:

$$lca(v, w) \text{ is a proper ancestor of } x$$
$$\Leftrightarrow$$
$$lca(v', w') \text{ is a proper ancestor of } x',$$

---

[1]http://www.inf.unibz.it/dis/projects/tree-edit-distance

where $lca(\mathsf{v}, \mathsf{w})$ denotes the least common ancestor of the nodes v and w.

The *constrained edit distance* between two trees is defined as the minimum cost mapping between the nodes of the trees that satisfies the constrained edit mapping.

Example 3.4   Figure 3.7 shows two trees T and T'. We compute the unconstrained and the constrained edit distance assuming a unit cost model. The *unconstrained* edit mapping between the trees is $M = \{(a,a), (d,d), (e,e), (c,i), (f,f)(g,g)\}$ (dotted lines) leading to a minimum cost edit sequence that renames c to i, deletes b, and inserts h; the unconstrained edit distance is $ted(T, T') = 3$.

In the *constrained* edit mapping M_c (dashed lines), the alignment (e, e) is forbidden since it violates the fourth condition: $lca(e, f)$ in T is a; a is a proper ancestor of d in T; assume (e, e), (f, f), $(d, d) \in M_c$; $lca(e, f)$ in T' is h, but h is not a proper ancestor of d in T'. Thus the constrained edit mapping is $M_c = \{(a,a), (d,d), (c,i), (f,f)(g,g)\}$, resulting in a minimum cost edit sequence that renames c to i, deletes nodes b and e, and inserts nodes h and e; the constrained edit distance is $cted(T, T') = 5$.

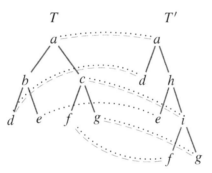

Figure 3.7: Constrained edit mapping.

The additional constraint limits the number of allowable edit mappings and reduces the complexity of the problem. The constrained edit distance is computed in $O(n^2)$ time in the number n of nodes in the larger tree. Since some of the alignments that are allowed in the unconstrained edit mapping are forbidden in the constrained edit mapping, the resulting constrained edit script may be suboptimal with respect to the unconstrained edit script.

3.2.4   UNORDERED TREE EDIT DISTANCE

So far we have assumed the ordered edit distance, i.e., the order of the children matters and two trees are different if the order of their children differs. The tree edit distance problem is NP-complete [Zhang et al., 1992] if the sibling order is ignored since after each edit step all tree permutations must be considered. The tree edit distance that ignores the sibling order is the *unordered tree edit distance*. It is defined as the minimum cost of a sequence of edit operations on ordered trees, where each edit operation is optionally preceded or followed by zero cost permutations.

Let T_x and T_y be ordered trees, $s = (T_1 = T_x, T_2, \ldots, T_k = T_y)$, $k \geq 2$, a sequence of ordered trees, $\pi_s \in \Pi(T_1) \times \Pi(T_2) \times \ldots \times \Pi(T_k)$ a permutation of the trees in s, and $\pi_{s,i}(T_i)$ the permutation of tree T_i in π_s. The *unordered tree edit distance* (uted) between T_x and T_y is defined as

$$\text{uted}(T_x, T_y) = \min_{s, \pi_s} \sum_{i=1}^{|s|-1} \text{ted}(\pi_{s,i}(T_i), T_{i+1}).$$

Finding the permutations of two ordered trees that yield the smallest tree edit distance is non-trivial, and it is obviously not feasible to compute the edit distance between all permutations of two ordered trees.

As an alternative, consider an approach that sorts the siblings of both trees by their string labels. This heuristic fails for the ordered tree edit distance. When the siblings of a tree are sorted, the subtrees rooted in the siblings are also sorted. Therefore two subtrees that should match may appear in a different order in the two sorted trees, for example, because the root nodes of the subtrees have different labels in the two trees. The ordered tree edit distance restores the subtree order and moves back subtrees node by node. A subtree can be of size $O(n)$, where n is the number of tree nodes. Thus, even if the unordered tree edit distance is zero or a small constant (for example, a single renamed node), the tree edit distance between the respective sorted trees may be $O(n)$.

Example 3.5   Consider the trees in Figure 3.8(a). The two children of the root node have the same label, and the label sort is not unique. Although both trees are sorted, the subtrees t_1 and t_2 are swapped in the two trees. The unordered tree edit distance is zero since the trees differ only in the sibling order. The ordered tree edit distance is roughly the tree size since the subtrees t_1 and t_2 must be moved back node by node. In Figure 3.8(b) the unordered tree edit distance is 1 (renaming the root node of t_1 from a to c), but the ordered tree edit distance is $O(n)$ since the renaming changes the subtree order in the sorted tree. In Figure 3.8(c) the ordered tree edit distance cannot insert node a with children b and d into the left tree since b and d are not consecutive siblings; the subtree order must be restored before the insert can take place. The unordered tree edit distance is 1 since a is inserted in a permutation of the left tree in which b and d are consecutive siblings.

Unordered Edit Mapping   An alternative definition of the unordered tree edit distance is based on an edit mapping. Let ϵ be the empty node and $N_\epsilon(T) = N(T) \cup \{\epsilon\}$. $M \subseteq N_\epsilon(T) \times N_\epsilon(T')$ is an *unordered edit mapping between T and T'* iff

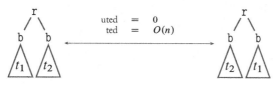

(a) Non-unique sorting.

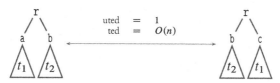

(b) Node rename and sorting.

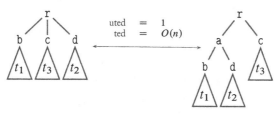

(c) Node insertion and sorting.

Figure 3.8: Tree sorting changes the subtree order.

1. each node is mapped:

   (a) $\forall v[v \in T \Leftrightarrow \exists v'((v, v') \in M)]$

   (b) $\forall v'[v' \in T' \Leftrightarrow \exists v((v, v') \in M)]$

   (c) $(\epsilon, \epsilon) \notin M$

2. all pairs of non-empty nodes $(v, v'), (w, w') \in M$ satisfy the following conditions:

   (a) $v = w \Leftrightarrow v' = w'$ (one-to-one condition)

   (b) v is an ancestor of $w \Leftrightarrow v'$ is an ancestor of w' (ancestor condition)

The unordered edit mapping differs from the ordered edit mapping only in the ordering condition that is missing in the unordered version. The unordered tree edit distance is defined as the minimum cost unordered edit mapping between two trees.

Computation of the Unordered Tree Edit Distance   The unordered tree edit distance problem is NP-hard [Zhang et al., 1992]. It was further shown to be MAX SNP-hard [Zhang and Jiang,

1994], i.e., there is no polynomial time approximation scheme (PTAS) for the unordered tree edit distance (unless NP=P) and no polynomial time algorithm can approximate the optimal solution within a factor of $1 + \epsilon$ for a given $\epsilon > 0$. For the unit cost model, Akutsu et al. [2013] show that the optimal solution can be approximated in polynomial time within a factor of $2h + 2$, where h is the maximum height of the input trees.

Shasha et al. [1994] propose an exhaustive search algorithm for the unordered tree edit distance, Horesh et al. [2006] and Higuchi et al. [2011] present A* algorithms. Akutsu et al. [2012] combine dynamic programming, exhaustive search, and maximum weighted bipartite matching to obtain an $O(1.26^{n+m})$ time algorithm for the unordered tree edit distance, where n and m are the numbers of nodes in the two input trees. Akutsu et al. [2011] develop a fixed-parameter tractable (FPT) algorithm that decides in $O(2.62^\tau \cdot poly(n))$ time if two trees with n nodes are within unit cost tree edit distance τ; this also implies that for a fixed threshold τ the decision can be made in polynomial time in the size of the input trees.

3.3   FURTHER READINGS

String Edit Distance Variants   By choosing specific cost models, the edit distance turns into other well known distance functions. If only replacements are allowed (i.e., the costs are $c_{rep} = 1$, $c_{ins} = c_{del} = \infty$) the edit distance is equivalent to the Hamming distance [Hamming, 1950]. The Hamming distance between two strings s_1 and s_2 ranges between zero for identical strings and the length of the two strings if they are of the same length; for strings of different length it is infinite.

Also the longest common subsequence [Apostolico and Galil, 1987, Needleman and Wunsch, 1970], LCS(s_1, s_2), between two strings is related to the edit distance. For a cost model that disallows replacement ($c_{rep} = \infty$, $c_{ins} = c_{del} = 1$), the longest common subsequence is defined as LCS(s_1, s_2) $= \frac{|s_1| + |s_2| - \text{sed}(s_1, s_2)}{2}$, where $|s_1|$ and $|s_2|$ are the number of characters in the strings s_1 and s_2, respectively.

A frequent typo is the character transposition, for example, `Peter` is misspelled as `Petre`. Two operations (e.g., two character replacements) are required to correct this error. An extension of the edit distance allows character transposition as a single operation with cost c_{trans}. This allows character transpositions to be cheaper than a sequence of two operations. This extension adds an additional line to the minimum in the recursive formula of the edit distance (cf. Section 3.1.2): sed($s_1[i..i-2], s_2[j..j-2]$) $+ c_{trans}$, where $c_{trans} = \infty$ if $s_1[i-1] \neq s_2[j]$ or $s_1[i] \neq s_2[j-1]$. Runtime and space complexity of the edit distance algorithm do not change.

Non-Edit-Based String Distances   In addition to the edit distance, other distance measures between strings have been proposed. The Jaro-Winkler distance [Winkler, 1990] is based on matching characters between two strings; it is not a metric like the edit distance. Phonetic algorithms, like Soundex and Metaphone, transform a string into a code that represents the pronunciation of the string. The goal is to map misspelled versions of a string to the same code as the correct string and thus match strings with small differences. Phonetic algorithms are optimized for a specific language, for example, Soundex and Metaphone work best for English, Kölner Phonetik is tuned to German. Soundex is implemented in commercial database systems.

Variants of the Tree Edit Distance   Other variants of the tree edit distances that can be computed in $O(n^2)$ time include the top-down distance [Selkow, 1977, Yang, 1991] and the alignment distance [Jiang et al., 1995]; a survey can be found in Bille [2005]. The RWS-Diff algorithm by Finis et al. [2013] is a heuristic that runs in $O(n \log n)$ time and also supports edit operations on subtrees. The bottom-up distance [Valiente, 2001] runs in linear time. It matches the largest common subforest of two trees, starting with the leaf nodes; if the leaves are different, the inner nodes are never compared, leading to poor edit scripts. The TASM (top-k approximate subtree matching) algorithm [Augsten et al., 2010a] computes the top-k closest subtrees (w.r.t. the tree edit distance) of a small query tree with m nodes in a large document tree with n nodes in $O(m^2 n)$ time and $O(m^2 + mk)$ space.

Graph Edit Distance   The edit distance can also be defined on graphs [Sanfeliu and Fu, 1983]. In the database literature, the graph edit distance is typically applied to so-called simple graphs, which do not contain self-loops or multiple edges between nodes. Each node has a single label [Wang et al., 2012c, Zeng et al., 2009]; in some works also each edge has a single label [Wang et al., 2012a, Zhao et al., 2012]. The edit distance between two graphs is defined as the minimum number of edit operations on nodes and edges that transform one graph into another. The following operations are allowed: (a) Delete an isolated node (i.e., a node with no incident edge) from the graph, (b) insert an isolated node into the graph, (c) delete the edge between two nodes, (d) insert an edge between two disconnected nodes, (e) change the label of a node, and, in the case of edges with labels, (f) change the label of an edge. The graph edit distance was shown to be NP-hard [Zeng et al., 2009]. A recent survey of algorithms for the graph edit distance is given by Gao et al. [2010].

CHAPTER 4

Token-Based Distances

Token-based distances represent strings and trees as sets of tokens, and the distance is computed as a similarity between the token sets. If the tokens can have duplicates, the tokenization produces bags instead of sets. In the following sections we show how bags are transformed into sets, we discuss the set similarity measures underlying token distances, and present tokenization techniques for strings, ordered trees, and unordered trees.

4.1 SETS AND BAGS

The tokenization of a string or a tree may result in duplicate tokens. It is typically easier to deal with sets rather than bags. We discuss two approaches to transform bags into sets.

4.1.1 COUNTING APPROACH

In the counting approach, each duplicate in a bag is given an identifier, which is unique within the duplicates. The identifier is a counter which is 1 for the first appearance of an element and is incremented for each further appearance of that element in the bag. Formally, bag $B = \{x_1^{m_1}, x_2^{m_2}, \ldots, x_n^{m_n}\}$, where $x_i^{m_i}$ is an element that appears m_i times in B, is transformed to the set $S = \bigcup_{1 \le i \le n} \bigcup_{1 \le j \le m_i} (x_i, j)$. Under this transformation, the set operations on S ($\cup$, $\cap$, $\setminus$) give the same result as the corresponding bag operations on B.

Example 4.1 Consider bag $B = \{\#b, ba, an, na, an, na, a\#\}$. The corresponding set using the counting approach is $S = \{(\#b, 1), (ba, 1), (an, 1), (na, 1), (an, 2), (na, 2), (a\#, 1)\}$.

4.1.2 FREQUENCY APPROACH

The frequency approach transforms elements of a bag B to pairs (x, i), where $x \in B$ and the integer i is the number of appearances of element x in B. While in the counting approach the number of elements in the bag and in the corresponding set are the same, the frequency approach stores each element of B only once. This leads to a more compact representation of the bag.

Example 4.2 Consider bag $B = \{\#b, ba, an, na, an, na, a\#\}$. The corresponding set using the frequency approach is $S = \{(\#b, 1), (ba, 1), (an, 2), (na, 2), (a\#, 1)\}$.

4.2 SIMILARITY MEASURES FOR SETS AND BAGS

The more similar two sets are, the higher is the similarity value. All set similarity measures are based on the intersection between the sets. Each similarity measure has a distance counterpart, which is smaller when the similarity is higher.

We also discuss similarity measures between bags and use the following notation: $B_1 \uplus B_2$ is the bag union of B_1 and B_2; an element that appears n times in B_1 and m times in B_2 appears $n + m$ times in $B_1 \uplus B_2$. $B_1 \cap\!\!\!\!\cap B_2$ is the bag intersection; an element that appears n times in B_1 and m times in B_2 appears $\min(n, m)$ times in $B_1 \cap\!\!\!\!\cap B_2$.

4.2.1 OVERLAP SIMILARITY

The *overlap similarity* between two sets S_1 and S_2 is the cardinality of their intersection:

$$O(S_1, S_2) = |S_1 \cap S_2|$$

It ranges from zero (if the two sets have no common element) to $\min(S_1, S_2)$ if one set is a subset of the other, or the sets are identical. The *overlap distance* is defined as $H(S_1, S_2) = |S_1| + |S_2| - 2|S_1 \cap S_2|$ and ranges from $|S_1| + |S_2|$ (no common element) to zero ($S_1 = S_2$). The overlap distance is equivalent to the *Hamming distance* between bit vectors, where each bit position represents an element of $S_1 \cup S_2$ which is 1, if the element is present in the set. The Hamming distance between two bit vectors of equal length is defined as the number of positions at which the corresponding bits are different.

For bags B_1 and B_2 the overlap similarity is defined as $O(B_1, B_2) = |B_1 \cap\!\!\!\!\cap B_2|$ with $0 \leq O(B_1, B_2) \leq \min(B_1, B_2)$, the overlap distance is defined as $M(B_1, B_2) = |B_1| + |B_2| - 2|B_1 \cap\!\!\!\!\cap B_2|$ with $0 \leq M(B_1, B_2) \leq |B_1| + |B_2|$. The overlap distance is equivalent to the *Manhattan distance* between integer vectors, where each vector position represents a different element of $B_1 \uplus B_2$ and stores the number of appearances of that element in the bag. The Manhattan distance (also L_1 distance) between two integer vectors $(x_1, x_2, \ldots, x_n)$ and $(y_1, y_2, \ldots, y_n)$ of length n is defined as $\sum_{i=1}^{n} |x_i - y_i|$.

4.2.2 JACCARD SIMILARITY

The Jaccard similarity [Jaccard, 1901] normalizes the overlap similarity to values between zero and one. The *Jaccard similarity* between two sets S_1 and S_2 is

$$J(S_1, S_2) = \frac{|S_1 \cap S_2|}{|S_1 \cup S_2|},$$

where $J(S_1, S_2) = 0$ stands for no similarity and $J(S_1, S_2) = 1$ for identical sets $S_1 = S_2$. Different from the overlap similarity, which cannot distinguish $S_1 \subset S_2$, $S_2 \subset S_1$, and $S_1 = S_2$, the Jaccard distance reaches the maximum value of 1 only for $S_1 = S_2$ and is smaller than 1 for $S_1 \subset S_2$ and $S_2 \subset S_1$. The *Jaccard distance* $1 - J(S_1, S_2)$ is a metric, i.e., $1 - J(S_1, S_2) = 0 \Leftrightarrow S_1 = S_2$, it is symmetric, and the triangle inequality holds.

For *bags* B_1 and B_2 we define the Jaccard similarity as:

$$J_B(B_1, B_2) = \frac{|B_1 \cap B_2|}{|B_1 \uplus B_2| - |B_1 \cap B_2|}$$

Note that we did *not* normalize with the bag union. Whereas the set union counts the elements in the intersection only once, the bag union $|B_1 \uplus B_2| = |B_1| + |B_2|$ counts them twice. The normalization with $|B_1| + |B_2|$ is the Dice similarity defined below. The Jaccard distance between bags, $1 - J_B(B_1, B_2)$, is a metric.

4.2.3 DICE SIMILARITY

The *Dice similarity* [Dice, 1945] between two sets S_1 and S_2 is:

$$D(S_1, S_2) = \frac{2|S_1 \cap S_2|}{|S_1| + |S_2|}$$

The values range from zero (dissimilar) to one (identical). The Dice distance is defined as $1 - D(S_1, S_2)$. The Dice similarity for bags B_1, B_2 is defined analogously as $\frac{2|B_1 \cap B_2|}{|B_1| + |B_2|}$, the Dice distance for bags as $1 - D(B_1, B_2)$. The Dice distance is *not* a metric. In particular, the triangle inequality does not hold. For example, for the sets $S_1 = \{x\}$, $S_2 = \{x, y\}$, $S_3 = \{y\}$: $1 - D(S_1, S_3) = 1, 1 - D(S_1, S_2) = 1 - D(S_2, S_3) = 1/3$.

4.2.4 CONVERTING THRESHOLD CONSTRAINTS

The predicate in a set similarity query is typically of the form $sim(S_1, S_2) \geq \tau$, where $sim(S_1, S_2)$ computes the similarity between the sets S_1 and S_2, and τ is the threshold. Many algorithms for similarity queries compute intersections between sets, i.e., the overlap similarity. Since the overlap similarity does not take into account the sizes of the compared sets, the similarity values are difficult to interpret. For example, an overlap of 5 can indicate identical sets if the compared sets have only 5 elements each; but for large sets it indicates low similarity. Thus, it is difficult to choose a single overlap threshold for a set similarity query. The threshold may be too large for the smaller sets in the data and too small for large sets.

Jaccard and Dice similarity are normalized and take into account the set sizes. Intuitively, they return the percentage of overlap between two sets and make it easier to specify a similarity threshold. The following theorem transforms Jaccard and Dice thresholds to equivalent overlap thresholds. The overlap threshold must be computed for each pair of sets separately since it varies with the set sizes. There are also equivalences between similarity and distance constraints, i.e., any similarity query can be transformed to an equivalent distance query.

Theorem 4.3   *Given two sets S_1 and S_2 and an overlap threshold τ. The following equivalences hold between Jaccard, Dice, and overlap similarity.*

$$J(S_1, S_2) \geq \tau \Leftrightarrow O(S_1, S_2) \geq \frac{\tau}{1+\tau}(|S_1| + |S_2|)$$

$$D(S_1, S_2) \geq \tau \Leftrightarrow O(S_1, S_2) \geq \frac{\tau}{2}(|S_1| + |S_2|)$$

Between the similarity and distance pairs for overlap, Jaccard, and Dice the following equivalences hold.

Overlap similarity and distance:
$$O(S_1, S_2) \geq \tau \Leftrightarrow H(S_1, S_2) \leq |S_1| + |S_2| - 2\tau$$

Jaccard similarity and distance:
$$J(S_1, S_2) \geq \tau \Leftrightarrow 1 - J(S_1, S_2) \leq 1 - \tau$$

Dice similarity and distance:
$$D(S_1, S_2) \geq \tau \Leftrightarrow 1 - D(S_1, S_2) \leq 1 - \tau$$

4.3   STRING TOKENS

The tokens for a string s are typically substrings of s. In information retrieval scenarios, where a string is a document, the tokens may be individual words, phrases, or even sentences of the document. For shorter strings, for example, person names or addresses stored in the customer table of a database, overlapping tokens are used. We focus on tokens for shorter strings and discuss q-grams as a widely used token technique.

4.3.1   Q-GRAM TOKENS

A q-gram is a substring with q characters. The q-grams of a string are produced by shifting a window of length q over the string such that each character of the string appears in each window position. For the first and last $q - 1$ characters in the string the window does not fit within the string for some window positions. The window positions that extend beyond the string border are filled with a dummy character #. In the following definition, $s_1 \circ s_2$ denotes the concatenation of the two substrings s_1 and s_2, and a^n denotes the concatenation of n characters a.

Definition 4.4   q-Gram.   The *q-grams* of a string s are all contiguous substrings of length q of the extended string $\#^{q-1} \circ s \circ \#^{q-1}$.

Example 4.5 We compute the q-grams of the string $s = $ banana. For $q = 2$ the extended string is #banana#, the q-grams of s are #b, ba, an, na, an, na, a#. For $q = 3$ the extended string is ##banana##, the q-grams are ##b, #ba, ban, ana, nan, ana, na#, a##.

Note that the q-grams of a string are not unique. For example, the q-gram na appears twice in the string banana. The bag of all q-grams of a string s, $X^q(s)$, is called the q-gram profile of s [Ukkonen, 1992]. The q-gram distance is defined as follows.

Definition 4.6 q-Gram Distance. Given two string s_1 and s_2 with the q-gram profiles $X^q(s_1)$ and $X^q(s_2)$, the q-gram distance between s_1 and s_2 is the overlap distance between the respective q-gram profiles:

$$D^q(s_1, s_2) = |X^q(s_1)| + |X^q(s_2)| - 2|X^q(s_1) \cap X^q(s_2)|$$

The normalized q-gram distance between s_1 and s_2 is defined as the Jaccard distance between the respective q-gram profiles:

$$D^q_{norm}(s_1, s_2) = \frac{D^q(s_1, s_2)}{|X^q(s_1)| + |X^q(s_2)| - |X^q(s_1) \cap X^q(s_2)|}$$

The size of q-gram profile is $|X^q(s)| = |s| + q - 1$, i.e., the number of q-grams of a string s is linear in the length $|s|$ of the string. The computation of the q-gram distance boils down to the computation of the overlap between two profiles since the cardinalities of the profiles are computed in constant time from the string lengths. The overlap of two profiles $X^q(s_1)$ and $X^q(s_2)$, $n = \max(|X^q(s_1)|, |X^q(s_2)|)$, is computed in $O(n \log n)$ time by sorting the profiles and traversing them in a merge fashion.

The q-gram distance is used as a lower bound for the edit distance (cf. Section 5.3.2) or as a distance on its own. Different from the edit distance, the q-gram distance can also handle block moves well. For example, the strings $s_1 = $ James Wood and $s_2 = $ Wood James are at the normalized edit distance $sed_{norm}(s_1, s_2) = 1.0$, whereas the q-gram distance for $q = 3$ is $D^q_{norm}(s_1, s_2) = 0.58$, i.e., for the q-gram distance the strings have some similarity, while they are completely different for the edit distance. In other cases, the q-gram distance underestimates the similarity, e.g., for the following two string representations of the same phone number, $s_1 = $ +39-06-46-74-22 and $s_2 = $ (39 06 467422), $sed_{norm}(s_1, s_2) = 0.4$ and $D^q_{norm}(s_1, s_2) = 1.0$ $(q = 3)$.

4.4 TOKENS FOR ORDERED TREES

Tree decompositions provide an alternative to the edit-based distances discussed in Chapter 3. Tree decompositions split a tree into small pieces, and trees with many common pieces are considered similar. We first provide an overview of different tree decomposition techniques, before discussing properties and implementation of the pq-gram decomposition technique in detail.

4.4.1   OVERVIEW OF ORDERED TREE TOKENS

A *tree decomposition*, $X(T)$, is a set of subtrees or subtree sequences, also termed a *snippet*, of a possibly preprocessed tree T. The preprocessing typically extends the original tree with dummy nodes, yielding an *extended tree*. A dummy node is a node with a special label (∗), which is different from all labels in the original tree. The extension of the tree with dummy nodes is required for snippets that would otherwise extend beyond the border of the tree. A tree decomposition is used to define and compute the distance between two trees. Two trees are similar if their decompositions have many snippets in common. Different tree decompositions have been proposed in the literature and are described next:

- *Binary Branches* [Yang et al., 2005]: A binary branch is a snippet that consists of a node, its first child, and its right sibling. The preprocessing adds the following dummy nodes to the original tree T: a parent and a right sibling to the root node, a node after the last child of each node, and a child to each leaf. For each non-dummy node of the extended tree T^{bb} one binary branch is produced. The binary branch decomposition of tree T in Figure 4.1 produces six snippets, each consisting of two small subtrees with two and one nodes, respectively.

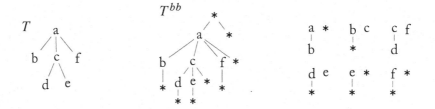

Figure 4.1: Tree decomposition with binary branches.

- *pq-Grams* [Augsten et al., 2005]: A *pq*-gram is a subtree that consists of an anchor node, q consecutive children, and the $p - 1$ closest ancestors of the anchor node. The preprocessing adds $p - 1$ dummy ancestors to the root, $q - 1$ dummy children before and after the children of each node, and q dummy children to each leaf node. For each non-dummy node of the extended tree T^{pq} all possible *pq*-grams are produced. The *pq*-gram decomposition of tree T ($p = 2, q = 3$) in Figure 4.2 splits the tree into 13 subtrees of the same shape.

- *Path Shingles* [Buttler, 2004]: A path shingle is a sequence of node chains. The tree is decomposed into all paths that contain the root node, the paths are ordered by the preorder numbers of their leaf nodes, and k consecutive paths form a path shingle of length k. The path shingle decomposition of tree T ($k = 2$) in Figure 4.3 produces five snippets, each consisting of two subtrees that are node chains.

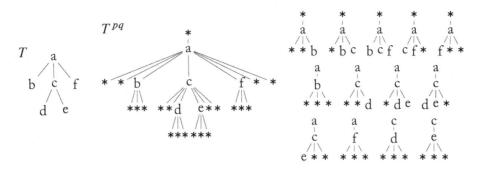

Figure 4.2: Tree decomposition with *pq*-grams.

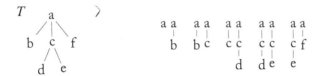

Figure 4.3: Tree decomposition with path shingles.

- *Valid Subtrees* [Garofalakis and Kumar, 2003]: The valid subtrees have different shapes and are produced in a sequence of parsing steps. In parsing step i, $i \geq 1$, a new tree T_i is obtained by contracting nodes of tree T_{i-1} into nodes of T_i. The parsing starts with $T_0 = T$ and stops if $|N(T_i)| = 1$. Nodes are contracted as follows: contiguous sequences of leaf children are split into blocks of length two or three, then the blocks are contracted; a leaf node is contracted with its parent if it is the leftmost leaf child that is not adjacent to any other leaf child; and finally, node chains are contracted into a single node. Each node of a tree T_i, $i \geq 0$, is a contracted subtree of the original tree T. A contracted subtree is called *valid subtree* and is a snippet of the decomposition.

  The valid subtree decomposition of tree T in Figure 4.4 produces 13 valid subtrees in total. The left column in Figure 4.4 shows the trees T_i that are produced in each parsing step by contracting nodes from T_{i-1}. Each node of a parse tree T_i represents a subtree in the original tree T. In our illustration, this subtree is encoded in the respective node labels. The right column shows the valid subtrees that are produced in each step. The valid subtrees of T_0 are the nodes of the original tree. The two contracted leaf nodes in Step 1 are connected with a dummy parent (i.e., a node that does not exist in the original tree) to form a tree. T_3 consists of a single node with a valid subtree that is equal to T.

Tree Parsing	Valid Subtrees

T_0

a
/ | \
b c f
/ \
d e

a b c d e f

T

a
/ | \
b c f
/ \
d e

Step 1: T_1 (a(b))

c f
|
((d)(e))

a   c   *   f
| / \
b   d e

Step 2: T_2 (a(b)(f))

(c(d)(e))

a   c
/ \   / \
b f   d e

Step 3: T_3 (a(b)(c(d)(e))(f))

a
/ | \
b c f
/ \
d e

Figure 4.4: Tree decomposition with valid subtrees.

4.4.2 THE PQ-GRAM DISTANCE

We discuss pq-grams as a representative tree decomposition technique and investigate the properties of a tree distance based on pq-grams. We show that, different from the tree edit distance, the pq-gram distance can be computed efficiently in $O(n \log n)$ time and linear space, and the pq-gram distance provides a lower bound for the fanout weighted tree edit distance. We illustrate pq-grams on the example trees in Figure 4.5, which shows a tree node as a pair of node identifier and label, e.g., the root node of T_1 is v_1 with label a.

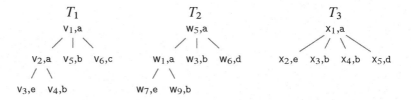

Figure 4.5: Example trees T_1, T_2, and T_3.

Intuitively, the pq-grams of a tree are all subtrees of a specific shape. To ensure that each node of the tree appears in at least one pq-gram, we extend the tree with dummy nodes. The pq-grams are defined as subtrees of the extended tree. Let T be a tree, and $p > 0$ and $q > 0$ be two integers. The *pq-extended tree*, T^{pq}, is constructed from T by adding $p-1$ ancestors to the root node, inserting $q-1$ children before the first and after the last child of each non-leaf node, and adding q children to each leaf of T. All newly inserted nodes are dummy nodes that do not occur in T.

Figure 4.6 shows the graphical representation of $T_1^{2,3}$, the $2, 3$-extended tree of example tree T_1.

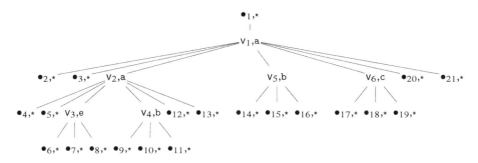

Figure 4.6: The extended tree $T_1^{2,3}$.

Definition 4.7 pq-Gram.   Let T be a tree, T^{pq} the respective extended tree, $p > 0, q > 0$. A subtree of T^{pq} is a *pq-gram* G of T iff

1. G has q leaf nodes and p non-leaf nodes,

2. all leaf nodes of G are children of a single node $\mathsf{a} \in G$ with fanout q, called the *anchor node*,

3. the leaf nodes of G are consecutive siblings in T^{pq}.

Example 4.8   Figure 4.7 shows some of the $2, 3$-grams of example tree T_1.

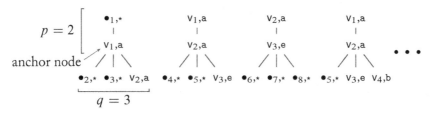

Figure 4.7: Some of the $2, 3$-grams of T_1.

Definition 4.9   Label Tuple.   Let G be a pq-gram with the nodes $N(G) = \{v_1, \ldots, v_p,$ $v_{p+1}, \ldots, v_{p+q}\}$, where v_i is the i-th node in preorder. The tuple $\lambda^*(G) = (\lambda(v_1), \ldots, \lambda(v_p),$ $\lambda(v_{p+1}), \ldots, \lambda(v_{p+q}))$ is called the *label tuple* of G.

Subsequently, if the distinction is clear from the context, we use the term *pq-gram* for both, the pq-gram itself and its representation as a label tuple.

Definition 4.10   pq-Gram Index.   Let X^{pq} be the set of all pq-grams of a tree T, $p > 0, q > 0$. The *pq-gram index*, $X_\lambda^{pq}(T)$, of T is defined as the bag of label tuples of all pq-grams of T, i.e., $X_\lambda^{pq}(T) = \biguplus_{G \in X^{pq}} \lambda^*(G)$.

The tables in Figure 4.8 show the 2, 3-gram index of T_1 and T_2, respectively. Note that pq-grams might appear more than once in a pq-gram index, e.g., $(a, b, *, *, *)$ appears twice in the index of T_1.

$X_\lambda^{2,3}(T_1)$	$X_\lambda^{2,3}(T_2)$
labels	*labels*
$(*, a, *, *, a)$	$(*, a, *, *, a)$
$(a, a, *, *, e)$	$(a, a, *, *, e)$
$(a, e, *, *, *)$	$(a, e, *, *, *)$
$(a, a, *, e, b)$	$(a, a, *, e, b)$
$(a, b, *, *, *)$	$(a, b, *, *, *)$
$(a, a, e, b, *)$	$(a, a, e, b, *)$
$(a, a, b, *, *)$	$(a, a, b, *, *)$
$(*, a, *, a, b)$	$(*, a, *, a, b)$
$(a, b, *, *, *)$	$(a, b, *, *, *)$
$(*, a, a, b, c)$	$(*, a, a, b, d)$
$(a, c, *, *, *)$	$(a, d, *, *, *)$
$(*, a, b, c, *)$	$(*, a, b, d, *)$
$(*, a, c, *, *)$	$(*, a, d, *, *)$

Figure 4.8: 2, 3-gram indexes of T_1 and T_2.

The pq-gram distance quantifies the similarity of two trees. It is based on the number of pq-grams that differ between the indexes of two trees.

Definition 4.11   pq-Gram Distance.   Let T_1 and T_2 be trees with pq-gram indexes $X_\lambda^{pq}(T_1)$, $X_\lambda^{pq}(T_2)$, $p > 0, q > 0$. The *pq-gram distance*, $D^{pq}(T_1, T_2)$, between the trees T_1 and T_2 is defined as the overlap distance between the respective indexes:

$$D^{pq}(T_1, T_2) = |X_\lambda^{pq}(T_1) \uplus X_\lambda^{pq}(T_2)| - 2|X_\lambda^{pq}(T_1) \cap X_\lambda^{pq}(T_2)|$$

The pq-gram distance is a pseudo-metric, i.e., for any trees T_1, T_2, and T_3, the following holds:

1. *non-negativity*: $\mathrm{D}^{pq}(T_1, T_2) \geq 0$

2. *reflexivity*: $T_1 = T_2 \Rightarrow \mathrm{D}^{pq}(T_1, T_2) = 0$

3. *symmetry*: $\mathrm{D}^{pq}(T_1, T_2) = \mathrm{D}^{pq}(T_2, T_1)$

4. *triangle inequality*: $\mathrm{D}^{pq}(T_1, T_2) + \mathrm{D}^{pq}(T_2, T_3) \geq \mathrm{D}^{pq}(T_1, T_3)$

The pseudo-metric properties are essential for many similarity search algorithms since they allow to efficiently prune the search space [Zezula et al., 2006]. Different from a metric, in a pseudo-metric non-identical trees may be at distance zero. An example of two different trees with the same pq-gram index is shown in Figure 4.9(a). The children of the root nodes are swapped. The pq-grams responsible for detecting the swapped children are those anchored in the root nodes of T and T' (the four leftmost pq-grams in Figure 4.9(b)). However, as the swapped children have the same label, these pq-grams are not affected by the swap and the pq-gram distance is zero.

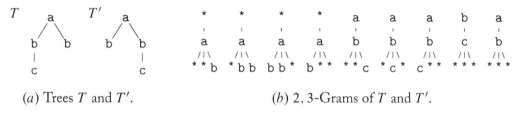

(a) Trees T and T'.   (b) 2, 3-Grams of T and T'.

Figure 4.9: Different trees with the same pq-gram index.

The pq-gram distance is the number of pq-grams that differ between two trees. The same number of different pq-grams may be considered a small change if the two trees are large, but a big change if the trees are small. We therefore define the *normalized pq-gram distance* that accounts for the tree size. The normalized pq-gram distance is 1 if two trees share no pq-grams and 0 for identical trees.

Definition 4.12 Normalized pq-Gram Distance.   Let T_1 and T_2 be trees with pq-gram indexes $X_\lambda^{pq}(T_1)$, $X_\lambda^{pq}(T_2)$, $p > 0, q > 0$. The *normalized pq-gram distance*, $\mathrm{D}_{norm}^{pq}(T_1, T_2)$, between the trees T_1 and T_2 is defined as follows:

$$\mathrm{D}_{norm}^{pq}(T_1, T_2) = \frac{\mathrm{D}^{pq}(T_1, T_2)}{|X_\lambda^{pq}(T_1) \uplus X_\lambda^{pq}(T_2)| - |X_\lambda^{pq}(T_1) \Cap X_\lambda^{pq}(T_2)|} \tag{4.1}$$

Example 4.13   Consider the normalized $2, 3$-gram distance between trees T_1 and T_2. The corresponding $2, 3$-gram indexes are shown in Figure 4.8. The bag-intersection of the two indexes is $\{(*, a, *, *, a), (a, a, *, *, e), (a, e, *, *, *), (a, a, *, e, b), (a, b, *, *, *), (a, a, e, b, *), (a, a, b, *, *), (*, a, *, a, b), (a, b, *, *, *)\}$, which yields $|X^{2,3}_\lambda(T_1) \cap X^{2,3}_\lambda(T_2)| = 9$. For the cardinality of the bag-union we get $|X^{2,3}_\lambda(T_1) \uplus X^{2,3}_\lambda(T_2)| = |X^{2,3}_\lambda(T_1)| + |X^{2,3}_\lambda(T_2)| = 26$. The normalized pq-gram distance is

$$D^{2,3}_{norm}(T_1, T_2) = \frac{26 - 2 \times 9}{26 - 9} = 0.47.$$

The normalized pq-gram distance ranges between 0 and 1 and is a pseudo-metric [Augsten et al., 2010b]. It is not obvious that a normalization maintains the pseudo-metric properties. For example, if we normalize by $|X^{pq}_\lambda(T_1) \uplus X^{pq}_\lambda(T_2)|$ instead of $|X^{pq}_\lambda(T_1) \uplus X^{pq}_\lambda(T_2)| - |X^{pq}_\lambda(T_1) \cap X^{pq}_\lambda(T_2)|$, the triangle inequality is not satisfied (cf. Section 4.2).

Below we state two important properties of pq-grams. Theorem 4.14 gives a bound for the size of the pq-gram index: it is linear in the number of tree nodes. Lemma 4.15 gives a bound for the number of pq-grams in which a node appears: it is small for leaves and increases with the fanout of a node.

Theorem 4.14 Linear Size of the pq-Gram Index.   *Let T be a tree with n nodes, $p > 0, q > 0$. The size of the pq-gram index of T is linear in the number of tree nodes: $|X^{pq}_\lambda(T)| = O(n)$.*

Lemma 4.15   *Let T be a balanced tree with all leaf nodes at the same distance h from the root node and a fixed fanout $f > 1$ for all non-leaf nodes. Further, let $v \in T$ be a node at level $l, 0 \le l \le h$. The number of pq-grams ($p > 0, q > 0$) that contain node v is as follows:*

$$\text{cnt}^{pq}(T, v) = \begin{cases} \frac{f^h - 1}{f - 1}(f + q - 1) + f^h & l = 0, h < p \\ \frac{f^p - 1}{f - 1}(f + q - 1) & l = 0, h \ge p \\ q + \frac{f^{h-l} - 1}{f - 1}(f + q - 1) + f^{h-l} & l > 0, h < l + p \\ q + \frac{f^p - 1}{f - 1}(f + q - 1) & l > 0, h \ge l + p \end{cases}$$

Lemma 4.15 assumes a completely balanced tree with a fixed fanout. If f is the *maximum* fanout of v and its descendants within distance $p - 1$, then $\text{cnt}^{pq}(T, v)$ is an upper bound for the number of pq-grams that contain v. The cost for changing a leaf node is $q + 1$, thus depends only on q. For non-leaf nodes the impact of p is prevalent, and we can control the sensitivity of pq-grams to structural changes by choosing the value for p. The difference between non-leaf and leaf nodes is relevant for hierarchical data where values higher up in the hierarchy are more significant.

4.4.3 AN ALGORITHM FOR THE PQ-GRAM INDEX

The core of the pq-gram distance computation is the computation of the indexes. We present a general algorithm for computing the pq-gram index and we show its linear complexity. A feature of this algorithm is that it can be efficiently implemented for trees stored in a relational database. We describe an implementation that requires only one scan over the relation that stores the trees. Efficient updates in response to structure and label changes in the underlying tree data are discussed by Augsten et al. [2006].

The basic idea of the pq-Gram-Index algorithm (see Algorithms 2 and 3) is to move a pq-gram pattern vertically and horizontally over the tree as illustrated in Figure 4.10. After each move the nodes covered by the pattern form a pq-gram.

Algorithm 2: pq-Gram-Index(T, p, q)

---

1   X_λ^{pq} : empty relation with schema $(labels)$;
2   *stem*: shift register of size p (filled with *);
3   $X_\lambda^{pq} \leftarrow$ index$(T, p, q, X_\lambda^{pq}, \text{root}(T), stem)$;
4   **return** X_λ^{pq};

We use two shift registers, *stem* of size p and *base* of size q, to represent the labels of a pq-gram; *stem* stores the labels of the anchor node and its ancestors, *base* the labels of the children of the anchor node. A shift register *reg* supports a single operation shift(reg, el), which returns *reg* with the oldest element dequeued and *el* enqueued. For example, shift$((a, b, c), x)$ returns (b, c, x). The concatenation of the two registers, *stem* $\circ$ *base*, is a label tuple in the pq-gram index, i.e., for *stem* $= (l_1, \dots, l_p)$ and *base* $= (l_{p+1}, \dots, l_{p+q})$ the label tuple in the pq-gram index is $(l_1, \dots, l_p, l_{p+1}, \dots, l_{p+q})$.

pq-Gram-Index takes as input a tree T, and the parameters p and q, and returns a relation that contains the pq-gram index of T. After the initialization, index calculates the pq-grams recursively, starting from the root node of T. Intuitively, index shifts a pq-gram shaped pattern vertically and horizontally over the tree, and the nodes covered by the pattern form a pq-gram. First, the label of the anchor node a is shifted into register *stem*, which corresponds to moving the pq-gram pattern one step down. Now *stem* contains the labels of a and its $p - 1$ ancestors. The loop at line 10 moves the register *base* from left to right over the children of a in order to produce all the pq-grams with anchor node a and calls index recursively for each child of a. Overall, index adds $f_a + q - 1$ label tuples to X_λ^{pq} if a is a non-leaf, otherwise 1 label tuple is added. The pq-extended tree is calculated on the fly by an adequate initialization of the shift registers (lines 2, 5, 14–16).

Example 4.16   Assume $p = 2$, $q = 3$, and the tree T_1 in Figure 4.5. The main data structures of the index algorithm are visualized in Figure 4.10. After the initialization,

---

Algorithm 3: index($T, p, q, X_\lambda^{pq}, \mathsf{a}, stem$)

5 *base*: shift register of size q (filled with *);
6 *stem* $\leftarrow$ shift(*stem*, $\lambda(\mathsf{a})$);
7 **if** a *is a leaf* **then**
8      $X_\lambda^{pq} \leftarrow X_\lambda^{pq} \cup \{stem \circ base\}$;
9 **else**
10   **foreach** *child* c *(from left to right) of* a **do**
11   *base* $\leftarrow$ shift(*base*, $\lambda(\mathsf{c})$);
12        $X_\lambda^{pq} \leftarrow X_\lambda^{pq} \cup \{stem \circ base\}$;
13        $X_\lambda^{pq} \leftarrow$ index($T, p, q, X_\lambda^{pq}, \mathsf{c}, stem$);
14   **for** $k \leftarrow 1$ **to** $q - 1$ **do**
15   *base* $\leftarrow$ shift(*base*, *);
16        $X_\lambda^{pq} \leftarrow X_\lambda^{pq} \cup \{stem \circ base\}$;
17 **return** X_λ^{pq};

---

index($T_1, 2, 3, \{\}, \mathsf{v}_1, (*, *)$) is called. Line 5 initializes $base = (*, *, *)$, and line 6 shifts the label of v_1 into the register *stem*, yielding $stem = (*, \mathsf{a})$. Since v_1 is not a leaf, we enter the loop at line 10 and process all children of v_1. The label of the first child, v_2, is shifted into register *base*, yielding $base = (*, *, \mathsf{a})$, and the first label tuple $(*, \mathsf{a}, *, *, \mathsf{a})$ is added to the result set X_λ^{pq}. Figure 4.10(b) shows the values of *stem* and *base* each time a label tuple is added to X_λ^{pq}. The indentation illustrates the recursion. The table in Figure 4.10(c) shows the result relation X_λ^{pq} with the label tuples in the order in which they are produced by the algorithm.

       pq-Gram-Index has runtime complexity $O(n)$ for a tree T, where n is the number of nodes in T: Each recursive call of index processes one node, and each node is processed exactly once. For the distance computation between two trees the index intersection is computed in $O(n \log n)$ time and $O(n)$ space using a standard sort-merge approach. Thus, the overall complexity of computing the pq-gram distance between two trees T and T' is $O(n \log n)$ time and $O(n)$ space, where n is the number of nodes of the larger tree.

4.4.4 RELATIONAL IMPLEMENTATION

The algorithms in the previous section are not optimized for a particular encoding of trees. In this section we present a scalable pq-gram index algorithm for all encodings of ordered labeled trees in a relational database that support efficient implementations of the following functions: a) sort the tree nodes in preorder, b) decide whether a node is a leaf, and c) decide the ancestor-descendant relationship between nodes. Examples of encodings that satisfy these criteria are the

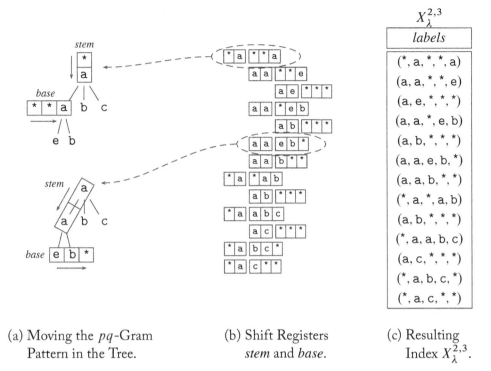

(a) Moving the *pq*-Gram
    Pattern in the Tree.

(b) Shift Registers
    stem and *base*.

(c) Resulting
    Index $X_\lambda^{2,3}$.

Figure 4.10: Illustration of the *pq*-gram index calculation.

interval encoding [Celko, 1994, 2004] and the Dewey encoding [O'Neil et al., 2004, Tatarinov et al., 2002]. The presentation of our algorithms assumes the interval encoding.

The interval encoding has been used to store and query XML data [Al-Khalifa et al., 2002, DeHaan et al., 2003, Grust, 2002, Zhang et al., 2001]. It stores the structure information of a node as a pair of integers (interval). We associate a unique index number with each tree in the set. A node of a tree is represented as a quadruple of tree index, node label, and left and right endpoint of the node's interval.

Definition 4.17 Interval Encoding.   An *interval encoding* of a tree T is a relation R that for each node $v \in T$ contains a tuple $(id(T), \lambda(v), lft, rgt)$; $id(T)$ is a unique identifier of the tree T, $\lambda(v)$ is the label of v, *lft* and *rgt* are the endpoints of the interval representing the node. *lft* and *rgt* are constrained as follows:

- *lft* < *rgt* for all $(id, lbl, lft, rgt) \in R$,

- $lft_a < lft_d$ and $rgt_a > rgt_d$ if node a is an ancestor of node d, and $(id(T), \lambda(a), lft_a, rgt_a) \in R$, and $(id(T), \lambda(d), lft_d, rgt_d) \in R$,

- $rgt_v < lft_w$ if node v is a left sibling of node w, and $(id(T), \lambda(v), lft_v, rgt_v) \in R$, and $(id(T), \lambda(w), lft_w, rgt_w) \in R$,

- $rgt = lft + 1$ if node v is a leaf node, and $(id(T), \lambda(v), lft, rgt) \in R$.

We get an interval encoding for a tree by traversing the tree in preorder, using an incremental counter that assigns the left interval value *lft* to each node when it is visited first, and the right value *rgt* when it is visited last. Figure 4.11 shows an address tree, where each node is annotated with the endpoints of the interval.

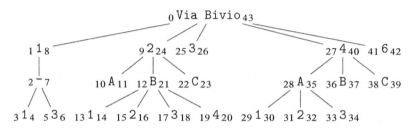

Figure 4.11: Address tree with interval encoding.

The interval encoding of a tree allows a scalable implementation of the algorithm pq-Gram-Index for a set of trees stored in a relation F with schema (*treeID, label, lft, rgt*). We define the following cursor:

```
cur = SELECT * FROM F ORDER BY treeID,lft
```

Then with a single scan all trees can be processed, and each tree is processed node-by-node in preorder.

Algorithms 4 and 5 are adapted for the interval encoding and the changes are highlighted. Instead of a tree, pq-Gram-Index gets a cursor as an argument. The function fetch(*cur*) retrieves the node at the current cursor position, next(*cur*) moves the cursor to the next node. Algorithm index processes all nodes of the tree in preorder, and when it terminates the cursor points to the root node of the next tree in the set.

Algorithm 4: pq-Gram-Index(*cur*, p, q)

---

1 X_λ^{pq} : empty relation with schema (*labels*);
2 *stem*: shift register of size p (filled with *);
3 $X_\lambda^{pq} \leftarrow$ index(*cur*, p, q, X_λ^{pq}, fetch(*cur*), *stem*);
4 **return** X_λ^{pq};

Algorithm index calls the following two functions:

Algorithm 5: index($cur, p, q, X_\lambda^{pq}, \mathsf{a}, stem$)

5   *base*: shift register of size q (filled with *);

6   $stem \leftarrow$ shift($stem, \lambda(\mathsf{a})$);

7   $cur \leftarrow$ next(cur);

8   **if** isLeaf(a) **then**

9     $\quad X_\lambda^{pq} \leftarrow X_\lambda^{pq} \cup \{stem \circ base\}$;

10   **else**

11     $\quad \mathsf{c} \leftarrow$ fetch(cur);

12     $\quad$ **while** isDescendant(c, a) **do**

13        $\quad\quad base \leftarrow$ shift($base, \lambda(\mathsf{c})$);

14        $\quad\quad X_\lambda^{pq} \leftarrow X_\lambda^{pq} \cup \{stem \circ base\}$;

15        $\quad\quad X_\lambda^{pq} \leftarrow$ index($cur, p, q, X_\lambda^{pq}, \mathsf{c}, stem$);

16        $\quad\quad \mathsf{c} \leftarrow$ fetch(cur);

17     $\quad$ **for** $k \leftarrow 1$ **to** $q - 1$ **do**

18        $\quad\quad base \leftarrow$ shift($base, ^*$);

19        $\quad\quad X_\lambda^{pq} \leftarrow X_\lambda^{pq} \cup \{stem \circ base\}$;

20   **return** X_λ^{pq};

- isLeaf(v): Returns true iff v is a leaf node, i.e., lft(v) $+ 1 =$ rgt(v).

- isDescendant(d, a): Returns true iff d is a descendant of a, i.e., lft(a) $<$ lft(d) and rgt(a) $>$ rgt(d) and *treeID*(a) $=$ *treeID*(d) and $\mathsf{d} \neq$ null.

Checking the ancestor-descendant relationship between nodes is a constant time operation for the interval encoding, while checking the parent-child relationship is more complex. In our algorithm this amounts to the same thing: When the loop on line 12 is entered the first time, c is the next node after a in preorder (or null). Thus, if c is a descendant of a, it must be a child. The recursive call in line 15 will process c and all its descendants, and sets the cursor on the next node after the processed nodes. Again, if this is a descendant of a, then it is a child. Thus, the while-loop of Algorithm 5 is equivalent to the for-loop of Algorithm 3.

4.5   TOKENS FOR UNORDERED TREES

The decomposition of a tree into snippets requires particular attention when the sibling order is not relevant. This section discusses techniques for unordered tree matching where the sibling order shall be ignored.

To facilitate the discussion, we use the following notation. The label of a node n is $\lambda(n)$. $C(n, T)$ denotes the *children of a node* $n \in T$, and $C_\lambda(n, T) = \{\lambda(x) : x \in C(n, T)\}$ is the corresponding bag of labels. We define a wildcard label "·" that matches all other labels. The *conditional labeling function*, $\lambda(n, C)$, returns the wildcard label if node n is not in a set of nodes C, i.e., $\lambda(n, C) = \lambda(n)$ if $n \in C$ and $\lambda(n, C) = $ "·" if $n \notin C$.

Given the tree decomposition $X(T)$, the *snippets of node* $n \in T$ are the snippets that contain at least two child nodes of n in the extended tree T^{ex}, i.e., $S(n, T) = \{s \in X(T) : |C(n, T^{ex}) \cap N(s)| \geq 2\}$. Note that the snippets of a node are affected by the sibling order.

Example 4.18   Consider example tree T in the figures of Section 4.4.1. The snippets of the root node are: the second and the third binary branch in the first row and the last binary branch in the second row in Figure 4.1; all pq-grams in the first row in Figure 4.2; the second and the last path shingle in Figure 4.3; and the first valid subtree of Steps 2 and 3 in Figure 4.4.

To simplify the notation, we represent a node by its label and a snippet by the concatenation of its node labels, e.g., the node $(1, a)$ is denoted as a, the snippet $((1, a), (2, b), (6, f))$ as abf.

A *conditional label tuple*, $\lambda(s, C)$, is the tuple of conditional labels for snippet s. $S_\lambda(n, T) = \{\lambda(s, C(n, T^{ex})) : s \in S(n, T)\}$ is the bag of all conditional label tuples of node $n \in T$. Notice that the conditional label tuples in $S_\lambda(n, T)$ convey only information about the horizontal structure (sibling relations), which are relevant for our discussion about order. The labels of the nodes that represent the vertical structure (parent-child relationship) are substituted by wildcard labels. Thus, conditional label tuples differ only if the labels of the siblings differ.

Example 4.19   Consider the figures in Section 4.4.1. The conditional label tuples of the root node of T for respectively, binary branches (bb), pq-grams (pq), path shingles (ps), and valid subtrees (vs), are:

- $S_\lambda^{bb}(a, T^{bb}) = \{\text{b·c, c·f, f·*}\}$

- $S_\lambda^{pq}(a, T^{pq}) = \{\text{··**b, ··*bc, ··bcf, ··cf*, ··f**}\}$

- $S_\lambda^{ps}(a, T) = \{\text{·b·c, ·c··f}\}$

- $S_\lambda^{vs}(a, T) = \{\text{·bf, ·bc··f}\}$

4.5.1   OVERVIEW OF UNORDERED TREE TOKENS

- *Embedded pivots* [Tatikonda and Parthasarathy, 2010]: An embedded pivot consists of two nodes and their least common ancestor, unless the least common ancestor is one of the two nodes. The children of each embedded pivot are sorted lexicographically. For a tree with n nodes $O(n^2)$ embedded pivots exist. Tree T in Figure 4.12 is split into 16 embedded pivots.

Figure 4.12: Tree decomposition with embedded pivots.

- *Windowed pq-grams* [Augsten et al., 2008]: Windowed pq-grams extend pq-grams to approximate the unordered tree edit distance. A windowed pq-gram is a snippet that consists of an anchor node, q children of the anchor node chosen from a window of size q, and $p-1$ ancestors of the node. The preprocessing adds the following nodes to tree T: q dummy children to each non-leaf node until the fanout is w, q dummy children to each leaf. For each non-dummy node of the extended tree T^{wpq} the windowed pq-grams are produced. For a tree with n nodes $O(n)$ windowed pq-grams exist. Tree T in Figure 4.13 is split into 16 windowed pq-grams ($p = 1$, $q = 2$, $w = 3$).

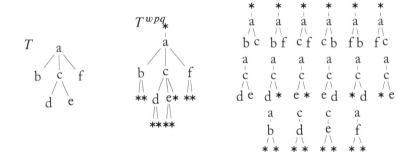

Figure 4.13: Tree decomposition with windowed pq-grams.

4.5.2 DESIRED PROPERTIES FOR UNORDERED TREE DECOMPOSITIONS

Based on our discussion of the unordered tree edit distance in Section 3.2.4, we identify three core properties that tree decompositions should satisfy when sibling order is ignored:

- *Preservation of Structure Information*: Each edge of a tree appears in the same number of snippets in the decomposition of the tree.

- *Preservation of Children Information*: The overlap of the snippets of two nodes from different trees should be the same as the overlap of their children.

- *Preservation of Sibling Information*: If the children of two parent nodes u and v are partitioned differently, i.e., the parent of some children is changed, the combined snippets of u and v are different.

In the sequel these properties are defined and error measures are introduced. We give examples that illustrate the effect of the decomposition properties in Section 4.5.4.

Preservation of Structure Information   The structure of a tree is given by its edges. The goal is to decompose a tree in such a way that all edges have the same impact on the tree distance. When an edge appears in one tree only, none of the snippets that contain that edge matches a snippet in the other tree, and the distance between the trees increases. Thus, the importance of an edge depends on the number of snippets that contain the edge. The structure information is preserved if each edge of the original tree appears in the same number of snippets.

Definition 4.20 Preservation of Structure Information.   Given a tree T with edges $E(T)$. The decomposition $X(T)$ preserves the structure information iff

$$\exists k \,\forall e : e \in E(T) \Rightarrow |\{s : s \in X(T) \wedge e \in E(s)\}| = k.$$

To measure the preservation of structure information we define the structure error. Let the *edge frequency* be the number of snippets in $X(T)$ that contain edge e, i.e., $\phi(e, T) = |\{s : s \in X(T) \wedge e \in E(s)\}|$; the average edge frequency of a set E of edges is $\bar{\phi}(E, T) = \sum_{e \in E} \phi(e, T)/|E|$. Then the structure error is defined as follows.

Definition 4.21 Structure Error.   The *structure error*, ϕ_ϵ, of an edge $e \in E(T)$ is defined as the relative error of its edge frequency with respect to the average edge frequency in T,

$$\phi_\epsilon(e, T) = |1 - \phi(e, T)/\bar{\phi}(E(T), T)|.$$

The structure error is the deviation of the frequency of a particular edge from the average edge frequency. The structure information is preserved if $\phi_\epsilon = 0$ for all edges of a tree.

Preservation of Children Information   The goal is to decompose two trees, T_1 and T_2, in such a way that the relative overlap between the snippets of two nodes, $n_1 \in T_1$ and $n_2 \in T_2$, is the same as the relative overlap between their children.

Definition 4.22   Preservation of Children Information.   Two decompositions $X(T_1)$, $X(T_2)$ preserve the children information iff for all pairs of non-leaf nodes $n_1 \in T_1$, $n_2 \in T_2$ it holds that $S_\lambda(n_1, T_1) \uplus S_\lambda(n_2, T_2) \neq \emptyset$ and

$$\frac{|C_\lambda(n_1, T_1) \Cap C_\lambda(n_2, T_2)|}{|C_\lambda(n_1, T_1) \uplus C_\lambda(n_2, T_2)|} = \frac{|S_\lambda(n_1, T_1) \Cap S_\lambda(n_2, T_2)|}{|S_\lambda(n_1, T_1) \uplus S_\lambda(n_2, T_2)|}.$$

We use the Jaccard similarity from Section 4.2 to quantify the children error.

Definition 4.23   Children Error.   Let $n_1 \in T_1$ and $n_2 \in T_2$ be two non-leaf nodes. The *children error*, ε, is defined as

$$\varepsilon(n_1, T_1, n_2, T_2) = |J_B(C_\lambda(n_1, T_1), C_\lambda(n_2, T_2)) - J_B(S_\lambda(n_1, T_1), S_\lambda(n_2, T_2))|$$

if $S_\lambda(n_1, T_1) \uplus S_\lambda(n_2, T_2) \neq \emptyset$, and $\varepsilon = 1$ otherwise.

The children error ε ranges from 0 to 1. If $\varepsilon = 0$ for all pairs of non-leaf nodes, the children information is fully preserved.

Preservation of Sibling Information   The goal is to decompose a tree such that the combined snippets of two nodes u and v are different if a child of u is moved to become a child of v.

Definition 4.24   Preservation of Sibling Information.   The decomposition $X(T_1)$ of a tree T_1 preserves the sibling information iff for the decomposition $X(T_2)$ of any tree T_2 that results from T_1 by moving a child n from its parent u to a new parent v the following holds:

$$S_\lambda(u, T_1) \uplus S_\lambda(v, T_1) \neq S_\lambda(u, T_2) \uplus S_\lambda(v, T_2).$$

The sibling information is relevant to detect changes that are not visible from the parent–child relationships between nodes. For example, if a node is moved to another parent with the same label, then the edges in the old and in the new tree have identical labels. Snippets that encode only parent-child relationships (e.g., snippets that consist of a single edge) cannot detect such a node move. If the moved node has siblings with different labels before and after the move, the node move can be detected using sibling information encoded in the snippets of the parent node. For instance, let n be a child that is moved from parent u to parent v, i.e., $C(u, T_2) = C(u, T_1) \setminus \{n\}$, and $C(v, T_2) = C(v, T_1) \cup \{n\}$. The node move is detected if at least one snippet changes, i.e., the union of the snippets of $u \in T_1$ and snippets of $v \in T_1$ is different from the union of snippets of $u \in T_2$ and snippets of $v \in T_2$.

Intuitively, the sibling information is measured as the number of different sibling pairs that appear in the snippets. The set of all (unordered) sibling pairs encoded by the snippets of a node n is $\mathrm{encpairs}(n, T) = \{\{a, b\} : \exists_{s \in S(n,T)}(a, b \in C(n, T^{ex}) \cap N(s)), a \neq b\}$. The set of all sibling pairs that can be formed for the children of a node n is $\mathrm{allpairs}(n, T) = \{\{a, b\} : a, b \in C(n, T), a \neq b\}$.

Not all sibling pairs are relevant for the sibling information. The same pair may be encoded twice, for example, in two different snippets and with different order. Snippets formed from the same sibling pair are duplicates and store redundant information. Sibling pairs with a dummy node provide no sibling information. The set of relevant sibling pairs is $\mathrm{encpairs}(n, T) \cap \mathrm{allpairs}(n, T)$.

We define the snippet recall and snippet precision to measure the preservation of sibling information.

Definition 4.25 Snippet Recall. Consider a node $n \in T$ with $f = |C(n, T)| \geq 2$ children. The *snippet recall*, ρ, is defined as the ratio of relevant sibling pairs encoded by the snippets of n to the number of all possible pairs, i.e.,

$$\rho(n, T) = \frac{|\mathrm{encpairs}(n, T) \cap \mathrm{allpairs}(n, T)|}{|\mathrm{allpairs}(n, T)|}.$$

With $f \geq 2$ children we can form $|\mathrm{allpairs}(n, T)| = \binom{f}{2} = \frac{f(f-1)}{2}$ pairs. $\rho = 1$ if all possible pairs of children of n are in the snippets of n, $\rho = 0$ if none of the possible pairs is encoded. Snippets with low recall may not encode relevant sibling pairs and thus miss node moves.

Definition 4.26 Snippet Precision. Consider a node $n \in T$. The *snippet precision*, π, is defined as the ratio of the relevant sibling pairs to the sibling pairs encoded by the snippets of n, i.e.,

$$\pi(n, T) = \frac{|\mathrm{encpairs}(n, T) \cap \mathrm{allpairs}(n, T)|}{|\mathrm{encpairs}(n, T)|}.$$

$\pi = 1$ if the snippets contain no dummy nodes. A low precision, i.e., many snippets with dummy nodes, decreases the weight of the original nodes.

4.5.3 THE WINDOWED PQ-GRAM DISTANCE

This section first introduces *windowed pq-grams*, which are independent of the sibling order and therefore well-suited for unordered tree matching. Then we define the windowed *pq*-gram distance and show that it is a pseudo-metric.

Constructing Windowed pq-Grams   The construction of windowed pq-grams is a 3-step process as illustrated in Figure 4.14:

1. *sort* the tree,

2. *extend* the sorted tree, and

3. *decompose* the extended tree into windowed pq-grams.

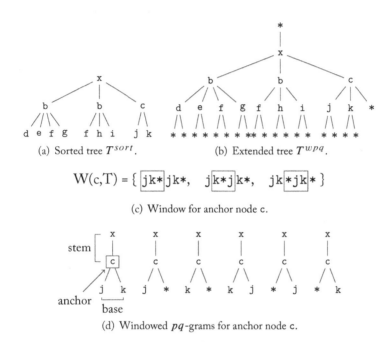

(a) Sorted tree T^{sort}.   (b) Extended tree T^{wpq}.

$$W(c,T) = \{ \boxed{jk*}\boxed{jk*}, \quad j\boxed{k*j}k*, \quad jk\boxed{*jk}* \}$$

(c) Window for anchor node c.

(d) Windowed pq-grams for anchor node c.

Figure 4.14: Construction of windowed pq-grams ($w=3$, $p=q=2$).

Dummy nodes ($\bullet_i$) have a special label, $\lambda(\bullet_i) = *$, which is the same for all dummy nodes. With $K(n, T)$ we denote the *sequence* of all children of node $n \in T$. Given two sequences a and b, $c = a \circ b$ denotes the concatenation of a and b, and $a \subseteq b$ denotes a being a (possibly non-consecutive) subsequence of b.

Definition 4.27 Window.   Given a tree T with extended tree T^{wpq}, a window size w, a node $n \in T$ that is a non-leaf in T, and the children sequence $K(n, T^{wpq})$ in the extended tree, a *window W over the children of node $n \in T$* is a consecutive subsequence of $K(n, T^{wpq}) \circ K(n, T^{wpq})$ of length w. $W(n, T)$ denotes the set of all windows over the children of n. If n is a leaf in T, no window is defined for n and $W(n, T) = \emptyset$.

Intuitively, windows are produced by shifting a pattern of length w over the children of a node. The nodes covered by the pattern form a window. Patterns are wrapped on the right side (concatenation of the children sequence).

Definition 4.28 Windowed pq-Grams.   Let T be a tree with extended tree T^{wpq}. An ordered tree G is a windowed pq-gram of T iff

1. G is a permuted subtree of T^{wpq} with q leaf and p non-leaf nodes,

2. all leaf nodes of G are children of a single *anchor node a* with fanout q,

3. $K(a, G) = K(a, T^{wpq})$ or $\exists W \in W(a, T)$ such that $K(a, G) \subseteq W$.

Conditions (1) and (2) in Definition 4.28 define the shape of the pq-grams, Condition (3) defines the nodes that appear in the bases. The base of a leaf anchor node consists of dummy nodes (left term in the disjunction), all other bases are (possibly non-consecutive) subsequences of a window.

Example 4.29   Figure 4.14(c) illustrates the construction of the window for node c. The concatenated children sequences is $K(\text{c}, T) = \text{jk*jk*}$, which gives the windows $W(\text{c}, T) = \{\text{jk*}, \text{k*j}, \text{*jk}\}$. Figure 4.14(d) shows all windowed pq-grams for $p = q = 2$ that can be formed for T^{wpq} and anchor node c. The respective conditional label tuples are $S^{wpq}_\lambda(\text{c}, T) = \{\cdots\text{jk}, \cdots\text{j*}, \cdots\text{k*}, \cdots\text{kj}, \cdots\text{*j}, \cdots\text{*k}\}$.

Dummy nodes, windows, and the concatenation of children sequences guarantee that each node of a tree is in the same number of bases produced from one tree, thus giving each node the same weight. Dummy nodes prevent a node from appearing twice in the same window when the two children sequences are concatenated. The concatenation guarantees that each node appears in all w positions of a window exactly once, independent of the number of left and right siblings. Only bases within windows are formed, thus each node is in the same number of bases.

Windowed pq-Gram Profile, Index, and Distance   Based on windowed pq-grams, we define an index and a distance for unordered trees.

Definition 4.30 Windowed pq-Gram Profile and Index.   Let T be a tree, $p > 0, w \geq q > 0$. The *windowed pq-gram profile* of T, $X^{wpq}(T)$, is the set of all windowed pq-grams of T. The *windowed pq-gram index* of T, $X^{wpq}_\lambda(T)$, is the bag of all label tuples of windowed pq-grams of T, i.e.,

$$X^{wpq}_\lambda(T) = \biguplus_{G \in X^{wpq}(T)} \lambda(G).$$

The following theorem shows that the size of the pq-gram profile is bound by $O(n)$ for a tree with n nodes, which makes pq-grams scalable for large trees (both in terms of memory requirements of the pq-gram index and in terms of computation of the pq-gram distance).

Theorem 4.31   Linear Profile Size.   *Let T be a tree with n nodes and let the base size $q > 1$ and the window size $w \geq q$ be constants. Then the size of the windowed pq-gram profile of T is linear in the tree size, $|X^{wpq}(T)| \leq nq\binom{w}{q}$. If all non-leaf nodes of T have fanout $f \geq w$, then $|X^{wpq}(T)| = (n-1)\binom{w-1}{q-1} + l$, where l is the number of leaves.*

The windowed pq-gram-distance between two trees is computed from the number of windowed pq-grams that the indexes of the compared trees have in common.

Definition 4.32   Windowed pq-Gram Distance.   Let T_1 and T_2 be two trees with index $X_\lambda^{wpq}(T_1)$ and $X_\lambda^{wpq}(T_2)$, respectively. The *windowed pq-gram distance*, $\mathrm{D}^{wpq}(T_1, T_2)$, between T_1 and T_2 is defined as

$$\mathrm{D}^{wpq}(T_1, T_2) = |X_\lambda^{wpq}(T_1) \uplus X_\lambda^{wpq}(T_2)| - 2|X_\lambda^{wpq}(T_1) \Cap X_\lambda^{wpq}(T_2)|. \qquad (4.2)$$

The windowed pq-gram-distance is a pseudo-metric, which means that it can be used to efficiently prune the search space [Zezula et al., 2006]. Different from a metric, in a pseudo-metric non-identical trees may be at distance zero, i.e., for any trees T_1, T_2, and T_3, the following holds:

1. *non-negativity*: $\mathrm{D}^{wpq}(T_1, T_2) \geq 0$

2. *reflexivity*: $T_1 = T_2 \Rightarrow \mathrm{D}^{wpq}(T_1, T_2) = 0$

3. *symmetry*: $\mathrm{D}^{wpq}(T_1, T_2) = \mathrm{D}^{wpq}(T_2, T_1)$

4. *triangle inequality*: $\mathrm{D}^{wpq}(T_1, T_2) + \mathrm{D}^{wpq}(T_2, T_3) \geq \mathrm{D}^{wpq}(T_1, T_3)$

To account for the size of the trees, the windowed pq-gram distance can be normalized by dividing the right-hand side of Equation 4.2 by $|X_\lambda^{wpq}(T_1) \uplus X_\lambda^{wpq}(T_2)| - |X_\lambda^{wpq}(T_1) \Cap X_\lambda^{wpq}(T_2)|$. This normalization preserves the metric properties.

We conclude with a theorem that asserts that tree sorting is a valid approach for windowed pq-grams. Sorting a tree changes the order in which its subtrees appear. However, the windowed pq-gram distance is independent of the size of the reordered subtrees. Only the windowed pq-grams that contain the root nodes of the reordered subtrees in the bases change. This core property qualifies windowed pq-grams for unordered tree matching and sets the windowed pq-gram distance apart from other distance measures such as the ordered tree edit distance.

Theorem 4.33 Local Effect of Reordering Subtree. *Assume a sorted tree T_1 is transformed into a tree T_2 by changing the order of the $f \geq w$ children of a node n. The reordering affects at most $O(f)$ windowed pq-grams, i.e.,*

$$|X_\lambda^{wpq}(T_1) \setminus X_\lambda^{wpq}(T_2)| = O(f).$$

Example 4.34 Consider the tree pairs in Figure 3.8. Subtree swaps due to non-unique sorting do not affect windowed pq-grams; the windowed pq-gram distance between the trees in Figure 3.8(a), which differ only in the sort order, is zero. Subtree swaps due to node rename (Figure 3.8(b)) and node insertion (Figure 3.8(c)) only change a constant number of windowed pq-grams, thus also the approximation error of the windowed pq-gram distance is bound by a constant. The error of the ordered tree edit distance is $O(n)$ in the number of tree nodes n for each of the three scenarios.

4.5.4 PROPERTIES OF WINDOWED PQ-GRAMS

This section shows that windowed pq-grams preserve the three properties introduced in Section 4.5.2, and we show the optimal choice of the parameters p (stem size), q (base size), and w (window size). Specifically, stems of size $p = 1$ have structure error zero (Lemma 4.36), and bases of size $q = 2$ have a smaller children error than larger bases (Lemma 4.38), but they detect the same node moves (Lemma 4.40). For $q = 2$ we provide snippet recall and precision (Lemma 4.41), and we provide a window size w that optimizes both recall and precision (Theorem 4.42).

To illustrate the properties of windowed pq-grams from Section 4.5.3 we also investigate three alternative and straightforward approaches to construct pq-grams:

- *All-permutation pq-grams:* All possible children permutations of length q form a base.

- *Consecutive children pq-grams:* The children are sorted, and each subsequence of length q of the sorted children forms a base.

- *Single leaf pq-grams:* Each child node is a base of length $q = 1$.

Similar to windowed pq-grams, $q - f$ dummy node children are added to each non-leaf node with fanout $f < q$, and each leaf is the anchor node of a single pq-gram with q dummy nodes in the base. We show that these approaches fail to meet the three requirements for tree decompositions.

Preservation of Structure Information and Stem Size   To preserve structure information, the structure error should be zero for all edges in the tree, i.e., all edges of the original tree should appear in the same number of windowed pq-grams. For $p = 1$ the frequency of an edge $e = (n, c)$ is equal to the number of bases in which child c appears. Thus, all nodes (except the root node) should appear in the same number of bases. This is not true for all-permutation pq-grams. There are $\frac{f!}{(f-q)!}$ permutations of length q over $f \geq q$ children and each child appears in $\frac{q}{f} \frac{f!}{(f-q)!} = O(f^{q-1})$ bases. Thus, for all-permutation pq-grams the pq-grams produced from children with many siblings disproportionately contribute to the total number of pq-grams. As a result, changes covered by these pq-grams are amplified, other changes are disregarded.

Example 4.35   Consider the trees in Figure 4.15. Both T_y and T_z are at the same distance uted $= 1$ from T_x (one rename operation), but at different distances for all-permutation pq-grams ($q = 3$):

- $|X_\lambda^{ap}(T_x) \uplus X_\lambda^{ap}(T_y)| = 282$
- $|X_\lambda^{ap}(T_x) \cap X_\lambda^{ap}(T_y)| = 80$
- $D^{ap}(T_x, T_y) = 122$
- $|X_\lambda^{ap}(T_x) \uplus X_\lambda^{ap}(T_z)| = 282$
- $|X_\lambda^{ap}(T_x) \cap X_\lambda^{ap}(T_z)| = 134$
- $D^{ap}(T_x, T_z) = 14$

The reason for the different distances is the number of bases in which the renamed nodes appear in the two trees. Node d is in a set of $f = 6$ children and appears in $\frac{q}{f} \frac{f!}{(f-q)!} = 60$ bases, i.e., the edge frequency is $\phi^{wpq}((\text{b}, \text{d}), T_x) = 60$. Node m has only a few siblings, and $\phi^{wpq}((\text{c}, \text{m}), T_x) = 6$.

The windowed pq-gram bases ($w = 3$, $q = 2$) that contain d and m are $\{\text{hd}, \text{id}, \text{de}, \text{df}\}$ and $\{\text{nm}, \text{om}, \text{mn}, \text{mo}\}$, respectively, thus $\phi^{wpq}((\text{b}, \text{d}), T_x) = \phi^{wpq}((\text{c}, \text{m}), T_x) = 4$, and the distances are identical: $D^{wpq}(T_x, T_y) = D^{wpq}(T_x, T_z) = 10$.

The following lemma shows that the structure error of windowed pq-grams with stem size $p = 1$ is zero.

Lemma 4.36   Optimal Stem Size.   *Let T be a tree and $X^{wpq}(T)$ be the set of all windowed pq-grams of T with $p = 1$ and $w \geq q > 0$. Then the structure error is zero for all edges in the tree, i.e.,*

$$\forall e \in E(T) : \phi_\epsilon^{wpq}(e, T) = 0. \tag{4.3}$$

Larger stems of size $p \geq 2$ explicitly store ancestor-descendant relationships of depth p. They give more weight to nodes with many children, and the structure error can be larger than

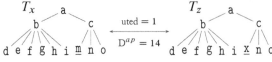

61 *pq*-grams change

7 *pq*-grams change

Figure 4.15: All-permutations *pq*-grams do not preserve structure information.

zero. In some situations it is beneficial to accept a non-zero structure error for the additional information encoded by stems. For example, for the address trees discussed in Section 4.6, larger stems are more effective.

Preservation of Children Information and Base Size   To preserve children information, the children error should be small, and it should be independent of the sorting order of the children labels. This is not the case for consecutive children *pq*-grams, where the children error varies along with the labels of the non-matching children. The children error is high if the non-matching children in the sorted children sequence appear between matching children, and low otherwise. Since the children error depends on the labels of the changed nodes, the distance for consecutive children *pq*-grams depends on the node labels, too.

Example 4.37   Consider the trees in Figure 4.16. We form consecutive children *pq*-grams for the children of x in T_x, T_y, and T_z, respectively. With $C_\lambda(x, T_x) = \{a, b, d\}$, $C_\lambda(x, T_y) = \{a, c, d\}$, and $C_\lambda(x, T_z) = \{a, b, e\}$ the children error is determined as follows ($q = 2$):

- $J_B(C_\lambda(x, T_x), C_\lambda(x, T_y)) = J_B(C_\lambda(x, T_x), C_\lambda(x, T_z)) = 2/3$
- $J_B(S_\lambda^{cc}(x, T_x), S_\lambda^{cc}(x, T_y)) = 0$ (no overlap)
- $\varepsilon^{cc}(x, T_x, x, T_y) = 2/3$
- $J_B(S_\lambda^{cc}(x, T_x), S_\lambda^{cc}(x, T_z)) = 1/2$ (50% overlap)
- $\varepsilon^{cc}(x, T_x, x, T_z)) = 1/6$

Though T_y and T_z are at the same distance uted $= 1$ from T_x, the distances for consecutive children *pq*-grams differ:

- $|X_\lambda^{cc}(T_x) \uplus X_\lambda^{cc}(T_y)| = 10$, $|X_\lambda^{cc}(T_x) \Cap X_\lambda^{cc}(T_y)| = 2$

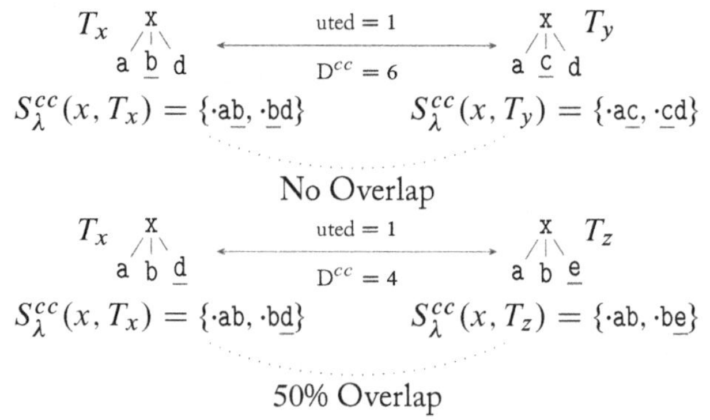

$$T_x \quad \overset{x}{\underset{a\ \underline{b}\ d}{/|\backslash}} \quad \xleftarrow[D^{cc}\,=\,6]{uted\,=\,1} \quad \overset{x}{\underset{a\ \underline{c}\ d}{/|\backslash}} \quad T_y$$

$$S_\lambda^{cc}(x, T_x) = \{\cdot a\underline{b}, \cdot b\underline{d}\} \qquad S_\lambda^{cc}(x, T_y) = \{\cdot a\underline{c}, \cdot c\underline{d}\}$$

No Overlap

$$T_x \quad \overset{x}{\underset{a\ b\ \underline{d}}{/|\backslash}} \quad \xleftarrow[D^{cc}\,=\,4]{uted\,=\,1} \quad \overset{x}{\underset{a\ b\ \underline{e}}{/|\backslash}} \quad T_z$$

$$S_\lambda^{cc}(x, T_x) = \{\cdot ab, \cdot b\underline{d}\} \qquad S_\lambda^{cc}(x, T_z) = \{\cdot ab, \cdot b\underline{e}\}$$

50% Overlap

Figure 4.16: Consecutive children pq-grams do not preserve children information.

- $D^{cc}(T_x, T_y) = 6$
- $|X_\lambda^{cc}(T_x) \uplus X_\lambda^{cc}(T_z)| = 10$, $|X_\lambda^{cc}(T_x) \cap\!\!\!\!\cap X_\lambda^{cc}(T_z)| = 3$
- $D^{cc}(T_x, T_z) = 4$

For windowed pq-grams ($w = 3$, $q = 2$), we get

- $S_\lambda^{wpq}(x, T_x) = \{\cdot ab, \cdot ad, \cdot bd, \cdot ba, \cdot da, \cdot db\}$
- $S_\lambda^{wpq}(x, T_y) = \{\cdot ac, \cdot ad, \cdot cd, \cdot ca, \cdot da, \cdot dc\}$
- $S_\lambda^{wpq}(x, T_z) = \{\cdot ab, \cdot ae, \cdot be, \cdot ba, \cdot ea, \cdot eb\}$
- $J_B(S_\lambda^{wpq}(x, T_x), S_\lambda^{wpq}(x, T_y)) = 1/3$
- $J_B(S_\lambda^{wpq}(x, T_x), S_\lambda^{wpq}(x, T_z)) = 1/3$
- $\varepsilon(x, T_x, x, T_y) = \varepsilon(x, T_x, x, T_z) = 1/3$
- $D^{wpq}(T_x, T_y) = D^{wpq}(T_x, T_z) = 10$

That is, the children error between T_x and T_y is the same as between T_x and T_z.

The following lemma shows that the children error for bases of size $q = 2$ is smaller than for bases of size $q > 2$.

Lemma 4.38 Optimal Base Size. *Let n be a node with f children and assume one of the following edit sequences that transform T_1 into T_2:*

1. *k insertions of new children of n*

2. *k children of n are renamed ($k \leq f$)*

3. *k children of n are deleted ($k \leq f$)*

For mutually different children labels and a window size $w \leq \min(|C(n, T_1)|, |C(n, T_2)|)$, *windowed pq-grams with bases of size 2, denoted as* $S^{wpq=2}(n, T_1)$, *have equal or smaller children error than pq-grams with bases of size* $q > 2$, *denoted as* $S^{wpq>2}(n, T_1)$, *i.e.*,

$$\varepsilon^{wpq=2}(n, T_1, n, T_2) \leq \varepsilon^{wpq>2}(n, T_1, n, T_2) \tag{4.4}$$

Preservation of Sibling Information and Window Size Single leaf pq-grams do not preserve sibling information and therefore fail to detect node moves to another parent if the ancestors in the old and the new position have identical labels. Ancestors with identical labels are frequent in data-centric XML (e.g., all title elements have the ancestors track and album in the XML of Figure 1.1). pq-grams with larger bases encode sibling information and can detect node moves since nodes with homonymous ancestors may have siblings with different labels. A node move is detected if at least one of the pq-grams changes.

Example 4.39 Single leaf pq-grams cannot distinguish trees T_1 and T_2 in Figure 4.17 since $X_\lambda^{sl}(T_1) = X_\lambda^{sl}(T_2)$ and therefore $D^{sl}(T_1, T_2) = 0$. The ancestors of the moved node d have identical labels, which yields identical stems. No sibling information is encoded, and snippet recall and snippet precision are zero. Windowed pq-grams encode sibling information and distinguish the two trees. The moved node d has a sibling c in T_1 but not in T_2, thus the snippet bcd exists only in T_1 and distinguishes it from T_2, and $D^{wpq}(T_1, T_2) = 8$ ($w = 3, p = 1, q = 2$). The snippets of node $(2, b)$ in Figure 4.17 are $S_\lambda^{wpq=2}((2, b), T_1) = \{\cdot cd, \cdot c*, \cdot d*, \cdot dc, \cdot * c, \cdot * d\}$. Snippets ·cd and ·dc are duplicates and all other snippets contain dummy nodes, thus encpairs$((2, b), T_1) = \{\{c, d\}, \{c, *\}, \{d, *\}\}$, allpairs$((2, b), T_1) = \{\{c, d\}\}$, snippet recall $\rho((2, b), T_1) = 1$ (the snippets encode all pairs of children of n), and snippet precision $\pi((2, b), T_1) = \frac{1}{3}$ (1 of 3 encoded pairs are relevant for detecting node moves).

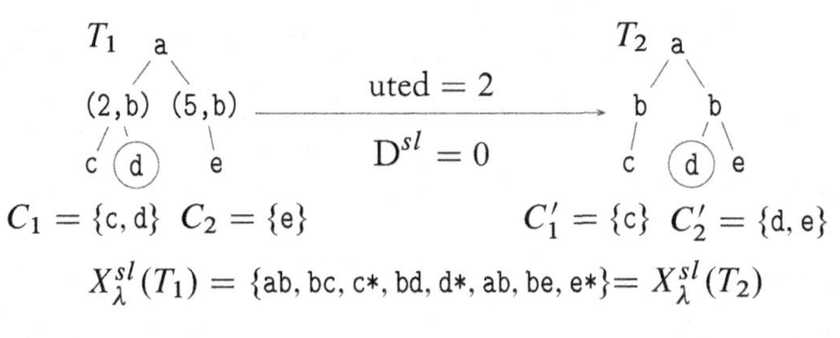

$$T_1 \quad a$$
$$(2,b) \quad (5,b)$$
$$c \quad d \quad e$$
$$\text{uted} = 2 \longrightarrow$$
$$D^{sl} = 0$$
$$T_2 \quad a$$
$$b \quad b$$
$$c \quad d \quad e$$

$$C_1 = \{c, d\} \quad C_2 = \{e\} \qquad\qquad C_1' = \{c\} \quad C_2' = \{d, e\}$$
$$X_\lambda^{sl}(T_1) = \{ab, bc, c*, bd, d*, ab, be, e*\} = X_\lambda^{sl}(T_2)$$

Figure 4.17: Single leaf pq-grams do not preserve sibling information.

Lemma 4.40 Node Move Detection. *Assume node* n *is moved from parent* u *to parent* v: $C(u, T_2) = C(u, T_1) \setminus \{n\}$ *and* $C(v, T_2) = C(v, T_1) \cup \{n\}$. *If for window size* w *the node move is* *detected by pq-grams with bases of size q > 2 then it is also detected by pq-grams with bases of size 2, i.e.,*

$$S_\lambda^{wpq>2}(u, T_1) \uplus S_\lambda^{wpq>2}(v, T_1) \neq S_\lambda^{wpq>2}(u, T_2) \uplus S_\lambda^{wpq>2}(v, T_2)$$
$$\Rightarrow S_\lambda^{wpq=2}(u, T_1) \uplus S_\lambda^{wpq=2}(v, T_1) \neq S_\lambda^{wpq=2}(u, T_2) \uplus S_\lambda^{wpq=2}(v, T_2)$$

Lemma 4.41 Recall and Precision. *Let n be a node with $f \geq 2$ children, $S^{wpq=2}(n, T)$ be the windowed pq-grams of n with base size $q = 2$ and window size $w \geq q$. Snippet recall, $\rho^{wpq=2}(n, T)$, and snippet precision, $\pi^{wpq=2}(n, T)$, are*

$$\rho = \begin{cases} 2\frac{w-1}{f-1} & w < \frac{f+1}{2} \\ 1 & w \geq \frac{f+1}{2} \end{cases} \quad and \quad \pi = \begin{cases} 1 & w < \frac{f+1}{2} \\ \frac{f-1}{2(w-1)} & w \geq \frac{f+1}{2} \end{cases}$$

Optimal Windowed pq-Grams The following theorem specifies the optimal parameters p, q, and w for windowed pq-grams such that the three properties for tree decompositions are maximally preserved.

Theorem 4.42 Optimal Windowed pq-Grams. *Assume a tree with fanout $f \geq 2$ for the non-leaf nodes. Windowed pq-grams with stem size $p = 1$, base size $q = 2$, and window size $w = \frac{f+1}{2}$ maximally preserve structure, children, and sibling information:*

    (a)   *Structure Error:* $\phi_\epsilon = 0$ *for all edges*

    (b)   *Children Error:* $\varepsilon \leq \begin{cases} \frac{k}{f} & \text{for rename} \\ \frac{2k}{2f+k} & \text{for insert} \\ \frac{2k}{2f-k} & \text{for delete} \end{cases}$

    (c)   *Snippet Recall:* $\rho = 1$ *for $w = \lceil \frac{f+1}{2} \rceil$*

    (d)   *Snippet Precision:* $\pi = 1$ *for $w = \lfloor \frac{f+1}{2} \rfloor$*

The optimal size of w depends on the fanout f. For a tree that consists only of the root node and $n - 1$ leaves, the optimal value is $w = (f + 1)/2 = O(n)$. Even in this case, the optimal windowed pq-gram profile cannot grow larger than $O(n^2)$ since for $q = 2$ and $f \geq w$ the profile size is $|X^{wpq}(T)| = (n - 1)(w - 1) + l$ (cf. Theorem 4.31).

Choosing bases of size $q > 2$ can be useful despite the higher base error. For example, larger bases give more weight to changes in the leaf nodes: The number of windowed pq-grams that are affected by a leaf change only depends on the number of bases in which the changed node appears (the number of stems is always one for leaves), and the number of affected bases increases with q. For trees with fanout $f = O(n)$ (see above), bases of size $q > 2$ in combination with the optimal window size $w = (f + 1)/2$ lead to large profiles. In this case it is not efficient to use the optimal window size, but a smaller constant must be used.

4.5.5 BUILDING THE WINDOWED PQ-GRAM INDEX

Algorithm 6 computes the windowed pq-gram profile X^{wpq} for $q = 2$ by recursively traversing the tree T in preorder. The algorithm is initialized with the root node n of T, the window size w, a stem of dummy nodes $(\bullet_1, \ldots, \bullet_p)$, and the empty profile $X^{wpq} = \emptyset$. Whenever the last child (in document order) of a node is reached, the children are sorted (dummy nodes to the end), and the windowed pq-grams are produced. The runtime is $O(n + f_{max} \log f_{max})$ for documents with n nodes, a maximal fanout of f_{max}, and constant window size.

Algorithm 6: getPQGrams$(T, n, w, \text{stem}, X^{wpq})$

---

1   stem $\leftarrow$ dequeue-first-element(stem) $\circ$ n;
2   **if** n *is a leaf* **then return** $X^{wpq} \cup \{(T, \text{stem} \circ (\bullet, \bullet)\}$;
3   C $\leftarrow \emptyset$;
4   **foreach** *child c of n* **do**
5   C $\leftarrow$ C $\cup \{c\}$;
6      $X^{wpq} \leftarrow X^{wpq} \cup$ getPQGrams$(T, c, w, \text{stem}, X^{wpq})$;
7   C $\leftarrow$ C $\cup \bigcup_{i=1}^{w-f} \{\bullet\}$;
8   $a \leftarrow$ sort-by-label(C);
9   **for** $i \leftarrow 0$ **to** $|a| - 1$ **do**
10   **for** $j \leftarrow i + 1$ **to** $i + w - 1$ **do**
11        $X^{wpq} \leftarrow X^{wpq} \cup \{(T, \text{stem} \circ a[i] \circ a[j \mod |a|])\}$;

12   **return** X^{wpq};

The index, X_λ^{wpq}, is computed by aggregating and counting the label tuples of the windowed pq-grams in the profile: $X_\lambda^{wpq} \leftarrow \gamma_{tid, \lambda(pqg); \text{COUNT}(*) \to freq}(X^{wpq})$, where γ is the grouping operator. The runtime is $O(n \log n)$ (sorting the profile of size $O(n)$). The index of a forest is the union of the indexes of its trees.

To deal with node labels of different length, such as element names and text values in XML documents, we use a fingerprint hash function that maps a string s to a hash value $h(s)$ of fixed length that is unique with a high probability (e.g., the Karp-Rabin fingerprint function [Karp and Rabin, 1987]). Instead of storing the label tuples of windowed pq-grams, we store the concatenation of the hashed labels. Note that the only operation we need to perform on the labels is to check equality.

Example 4.43   Figure 4.18 shows an example hash function and part of the windowed pq-gram indexes of the two XML documents in Figure 1.1, the music albums from the song lyric store (T_{LS}) and the CD warehouse (T_{WH}). We choose $p = q = 2$, $w = 3$, $\lambda(\bullet) = (*, *)$. The label tuple $((*, *), (\text{album}, \epsilon), (\text{track}, \epsilon), (\text{track}, \epsilon))$ with hash value 9999 4100 3200 3200 appears twice in the index of T_{LS} and has two matches in the other index. The label tuple $((\text{album}, \epsilon), (\text{year}, 2000), (*, *), (*, *))$ with the hash value 4100 5497 9999 9999 appears only once in the index of T_{LS} and has no match in the index of T_{WH}.

s	$h(s)$
*	99
ϵ	00
album	41
track	32
title	02
artist	11
year	54
price	19
So far away	67
Mark	86
John	15
2000	97
15	73
Wish you where here	42
Roger	26
Dave	09
Nick	37

(a) Hash Function.

tid	pqg	freq
...	...	...
T_{LS}	9999 4100 3200 5497	2
T_{LS}	9999 4100 3200 3200	2
T_{LS}	9999 4100 5497 3200	2
T_{LS}	4100 5497 9999 9999	1
T_{LS}	4100 3200 0267 1186	1
T_{LS}	4100 3200 0267 1115	1
T_{LS}	4100 3200 1186 1115	1
...	...	...

(b) pq-Gram Index of the Song Lyric Store.

tid	pqg	freq
...	...	...
T_{WH}	9999 4100 3200 3200	2
T_{WH}	9999 4100 3200 1973	2
T_{WH}	9999 4100 1973 3200	2
T_{WH}	4100 1973 9999 9999	1
T_{WH}	4100 3200 0267 1115	1
T_{WH}	4100 3200 0267 1186	1
T_{WH}	4100 3200 1115 1186	1
...	...	...

(c) pq-Gram Index of the CD Warehouse.

Figure 4.18: Implementation of the windowed pq-gram index.

4.6   DISCUSSION: PROPERTIES OF TREE TOKENS

We test the effectiveness of token distances on address trees generated from address information of Bolzano.[1] This dataset consists of two sets of trees, L and R, and each tree (called address

---
[1]http://www.cosy.sbg.ac.at/~augsten/tods10/

tree) represents a street of the city of Bolzano with all its addresses. Each root-leaf path in the tree represents a residential address. The root node is the street name, the second level stores the house numbers, the third level the entrance numbers, and the fourth level the apartment numbers (cf. Section 1.1).

The trees are generated from two databases of the city administration that both store residential addresses. Although both databases cover the entire city, the residential addresses in the two databases differ due to spelling mistakes, missing addresses, street names that are spelled differently, and addresses stored at different levels of detail (e.g., with/without apartment numbers). Thus, address trees that should match are different. The tree set L consists of 299 trees with 52,509 nodes in total, reflecting 44,427 addresses; the set R consists of 302 trees with 52,509 nodes and 43,187 addresses.

Street matching is challenging since there is a large overlap between the labels of the trees. All labels (except the street name) are either numbers (house or apartment numbers) or single characters (entrance names, e.g., A, B). A tree decomposition may produce identical snippets at different positions in a tree (for example, a snippet 123 may be produced from three consecutive house numbers *or* apartment numbers), and all trees produce similar snippets.

The matching is done as follows. For each distance function D^x we compute a mapping $M^x \subseteq F_1 \times F_2$. Two trees $T_i \in F_1$ and $T_j \in F_2$ are paired, i.e., $(T_i, T_j) \in M^x$, iff T_i has only one nearest neighbor in F_2, namely T_j, and vice versa. We sort the trees and compute a mapping for the windowed pq-gram distance [Augsten et al., 2008], the ordered tree edit distance [Zhang and Shasha, 1989], the pq-gram distance [Augsten et al., 2005, 2010b], the tree embedding distance [Garofalakis and Kumar, 2005], the binary branch distance [Yang et al., 2005], single path shingles [Buttler, 2004], embedded pivots [Tatikonda and Parthasarathy, 2010], and the node intersection distance. The node intersection distance is a simple algorithm that completely ignores the structure of the tree. It is computed in the same way as the (windowed) pq-gram distance, the only difference being that the index of a tree consists of the bag of all its node labels. The correct mapping, M^c, contains all pairs of trees that represent the same street in the real world and is computed by hand. There are three streets in R that do not exist in L, thus $|M^c| = 299$ for the computation of precision and recall.

The results are shown in Table 4.1. In terms of overall effectiveness (F-measure) the windowed pq-gram distance outperforms all other distances. The closest competitor is the ordered tree edit distance with sorting. Windowed pq-grams are more effective than pq-grams. By increasing the window size, windowed pq-grams preserve more sibling information (which is relevant to distinguish similar trees) without increasing the children error. For pq-grams the base size q is a tradeoff between preserving more sibling information and increasing the children error. Table 4.1 shows the effectiveness of pq-grams for the best parameter setting that we found.

The other distance algorithms perform only slightly better or even worse than the simple node intersection distance. The tree-embedding produces many snippets that are single nodes and thus gives less weight to the tree structure than windowed pq-grams [Augsten et al., 2005].

Distance	Correct	Recall	Precision	F-Measure	Runtime
wind pq-grams ($w=8, p=2, q=2$)	248	82.9%	98.4%	0.900	24.9 s
wind pq-grams ($w=5, p=1, q=2$)	245	81.9%	98.8%	0.896	12.7 s
wind pq-grams ($w=3, p=2, q=2$)	240	80.3%	98.8%	0.886	7.4 s
ordered tree edit distance	247	82.6%	96.5%	0.890	669.0s
pq-grams ($p=3, q=2$)	237	79.3%	99.2%	0.881	4.4s
tree-embedding	206	68.9%	96.3%	0.803	6.9s
node intersection	197	65.9%	93.8%	0.774	2.2s
binary branch	193	64.5%	93.2%	0.763	7.1s
embedded pivots	165	55.1%	98.2%	0.707	344.4s
path shingles	73	24.4%	98.6%	0.391	7.8s

Table 4.1: Effectiveness of different tree distances for matching address trees.

Similarly, the binary branch snippets do not store the edges between a parent and its children (except the edge to the first child), leading to poor performance when many nodes in the trees have identical labels. Embedded pivots give a disproportionate weight to the root label: a quadratic number of snippets is produced from the root, while only a linear number is produced for each leaf [Tatikonda and Parthasarathy, 2010]. The root label is the street name, thus address trees with different street names are unlikely to be paired. This effect is even more pronounced for path shingles, where all snippets contain the root node.

We also tested variants of embedded pivots which store the level difference between the nodes in the snippet or select a subset of all pivots for which the level difference is within a threshold (1, 2, or 3) [Tatikonda and Parthasarathy, 2010]. For single path shingles we tested shingles of size larger than one. In Table 4.1 we only show the results for the winning variants.

4.7   FURTHER READINGS

In addition to the fixed-length q-grams discussed in Section 4.3, q-grams of variable length have also been proposed [Li et al., 2007, Yang et al., 2008].

The idea of pq-grams for trees has also been generalized to graphs to improve the efficiency of similarity queries based on the graph edit distance (cf. Section 3.3). Zeng et al. [2009] split a graph into so-called stars, which are trees consisting of a node and all neighboring nodes. Wang et al. [2012a] produce κ-adjacent trees, which are similar to stars, but consider all nodes within distance κ from the root node of the token tree, i.e., a κ-adjacent tree for $\kappa = 1$ is a star. The path-based q-grams proposed by Zhao et al. [2012] consist of all paths of length q in the graph.

CHAPTER 5

Query Processing Techniques

In this chapter we discuss filters, in particular lower and upper bounds, which are used to speed up similarity queries by reducing the number of expensive distance computations. We give lower bounds for the string edit distance and show their implementation in SQL. We provide an upper bound for the tree edit distance and discuss lower bounds for both the unit cost and the fanout weighted tree edit distance.

5.1 FILTERS

Often there is a preferable distance measure from the application point of view, but this distance is expensive to compute. Especially in a join, where all pairs of objects must be considered, it is essential that the query predicate is evaluated efficiently. Algorithm 7 shows a nested-loop similarity join which returns all pairs of objects (s_1, s_2) from the sets X and Y such that $\text{distance}(s_1, s_2) \leq \tau$. The number of calls to the (expensive) distance function is $|X| \times |Y|$.

Algorithm 7: $\text{nestedLoopNaive}(X, Y)$

---

1   **foreach** $s_1 \in X$ **do**
2   **foreach** $s_2 \in Y$ **do**
3   **if** $\text{distance}(s_1, s_2) \leq \tau$ **then**
4   **output** (s_1, s_2);

In many applications the result size of the similarity join is much smaller than the cross product, often even linear in the input size. Many of the object pairs, for which the similarity is computed, are very different from each other. This is where filters come into play.

Filters preprocess the input sets and produce a set of candidate pairs, which is a subset of the cross product, $C \subseteq X \times Y$. The distance function is then evaluated only on the candidate pairs. If the filter condition can be evaluated faster than the distance function, the overall join will be faster.

Filters place a pair $(s_1, s_2) \in X \times Y$ into the candidate set based on a fast guess. There are four possibilities for this guess, illustrated in Table 5.1. On true positives and true negatives the filter guess is correct. Candidates that do not qualify for the result set are *false positives*. Since the actual distance is computed on all pairs in the candidate set, false positives are removed. False positives increase the runtime, but do not affect the correctness. This is different for *false negatives*. A false negative is a pair that should be in the result set, but does not make it into the candidate set and is thus missed. Ideally, a filter produces no false negatives (to guarantee the correctness of the result) and few false positives (to increase the efficiency).

| | | Result Pair | |
		yes	no
Candidate	yes	true positive	false positive
Pair	no	false negative	true negative

Table 5.1: Error types of filters.

The filters discussed in this chapter do not produce false negatives, i.e., applying these filters in a join leads to the same result as executing the naive nested-loop join in Algorithm 7. We will discuss upper and lower bounds for the edit distance between strings and trees.

5.2   LOWER AND UPPER BOUNDS

For a given distance measure, a lower bound function produces a value that is within the distance value for any pair of input objects. Similarly, an upper bound function produces a value that is equal or larger than the distance value. That is, iff for any pair (s_1, s_2) of objects

$$\texttt{distance}(s_1, s_2) \geq \texttt{lowerBound}(s_1, s_2) \tag{5.1}$$
$$\texttt{distance}(s_1, s_2) \leq \texttt{upperBound}(s_1, s_2) \tag{5.2}$$

then $\texttt{lowerBound}(s_1, s_2)$ is a lower bound and $\texttt{upperBound}(s_1, s_2)$ is an upper bound for the function $\texttt{distance}$.

These properties of the lower and upper bound are used to rephrase the nested loop similarity join as shown in Algorithm 8. Before the distance is computed for a pair of objects (s_1, s_2), the lower and upper bound are evaluated. If the upper bound is within threshold τ, then also the distance is within τ, and we know that the pair is in the result set (true positive). If the lower bound exceeds τ, also the distance will exceed τ, and the pair is not in the result set (true negative). All other pairs are candidates and the distance function must be called to remove false positives. There are no false negatives.

An interesting observation about lower and upper bounds is that they can be combined. Let $lb_1, lb_2, \ldots, lb_n$ be lower bounds for a distance d and $ub_1, ub_2, \ldots, ub_m$ be upper bounds, then $lb = \max(lb_1, lb_2, \ldots, lb_n)$ and $ub = \min(ub_1, ub_2, \ldots, ub_m)$ are respectively lower and upper bounds for d as well. The new lower/upper bound is as tight as the tightest of the bounds lb_i/ub_j, $1 \leq i \leq n$, $1 \leq j \leq m$. Since the effectiveness of bounding functions often depends on the structure of the data, combining bounds leads to a more robust overall bound. Further, bounds can be applied in the order of their efficiency. The fast bounds are computed first. Only if the fast bounds are not tight enough, more expensive bounds are computed.

Algorithm 8: nestedLoopWithBounds(X, Y)

---

1 **foreach** $s_1 \in X$ **do**
2   **foreach** $s_2 \in Y$ **do**
3   **if** upperBound(s_1, s_2) $\leq \tau$ **then**
4   **output** (s_1, s_2);
5   **else if** lowerBound(s_1, s_2) $> \tau$ **then**
6   /* nothing to do */
7   **else if** distance(s_1, s_2) $\leq \tau$ **then**
8   **output** (s_1, s_2);

Only bounding functions that are evaluated faster than the distance function are useful. Then the similarity join with upper and lower bounds is typically much faster than the naive nested loop join. The use of lower and upper bounds in the similarity join is very appealing since the join can be computed faster without sacrificing the correctness of the result. Upper and lower bounds have been developed for the edit distance between strings and the edit distance between trees. We will discuss these bounds next.

5.3   STRING DISTANCE BOUNDS

5.3.1   LENGTH FILTER

A simple filter criterion is the length filter. The length of two strings s_1 and s_2 that are at edit distance $k = sed(s_1, s_2)$ cannot differ by more than k, since k insertions or deletions are required to get strings of the same length.

$$sed(s_1, s_2) \geq abs(|s_1| - |s_2|) \tag{5.3}$$

The length filter can be evaluated in constant time. Its effectiveness depends on the length distribution of the strings in the dataset. The filter is effective only for strings with different lengths. For datasets, where many string have similar lengths, many false positives will be produced for the candidate set.

5.3.2   COUNT FILTER

A more effective lower bound technique is based on q-grams. Intuitively, strings with a small edit distance share many q-grams. The number of common q-grams between two strings provides a lower bound on the edit distance. The common q-grams (intersection) are computed efficiently in $O(n \log n)$ time, whereas the edit distance requires $O(n^2)$.

We study how edit operations change the intersection of the q-grams between two strings s_1 and s_2. With $X^q(s_1)$ and $X^q(s_2)$ we denote the bags of all q-grams of s_1 and s_2, respectively.

In our examples we use $q = 3$. We start with a single edit operation that transforms s_1 into s_2, as illustrated in Figure 5.1(a). A single edit operation affects a single character, which in turn appears in q q-grams. Thus, a single edit operation affects q q-grams, which will no longer be in the intersection. For two strings s_1 and s_2 at edit distance 1 we get:

$$sed(s_1, s_2) = 1 \Rightarrow |X^q(s_1) \cap X^q(s_2)| = \max(|X^q(s_1)|, |X^q(s_2)|) - q \qquad (5.4)$$

	s_1	$|X^q(s_1)|$	s_2	$|X^q(s_2)|$	$|X^q(s_1) \cap X^q(s_2)|$
replace	peter	7	meter	7	4
insert	peter	7	peters	8	5
delete	peter	7	peer	6	4

(a) Single edit operation.

s_1	$|X^q(s_1)|$	s_2	$|X^q(s_2)|$	$|X^q(s_1) \cap X^q(s_2)|$
peter	7	meters	8	2
peter	7	petal	7	3

(b) Two edit operations.

Figure 5.1: Edit distance and number of affected q-grams.

We generalize the result for a single edit operation to multiple edits. Figure 5.1(b) shows examples for edit distance $k = 2$. We observe that the two edit operations between the string pair (peter, meters) change $kq = 6$ q-grams:

$$\text{peter} \rightarrow X^q(s_1) = \{\#\#p, \#pe, pet, ete, ter, er\#, r\#\#\}$$
$$\text{meters} \rightarrow X^q(s_2) = \{\#\#m, \#me, met, ete, ter, ers, rs\#, s\#\#\}$$

This observation, however, cannot be generalized. In the above example, the edits are far from each other in the string such that the affected q-grams do not overlap. When the q-grams overlap, fewer q-grams are affected since some of the q-grams are affected twice, as shown in the following example:

$$\text{peter} \rightarrow X^q(s_1) = \{\#\#p, \#pe, pet, ete, ter, er\#, r\#\#\}$$
$$\text{petal} \rightarrow X^q(s_2) = \{\#\#p, \#pe, pet, eta, tal, al\#, l\#\#\}$$

For the intersection it does not matter how different two q-grams are, and multiple affected q-grams count only once. As a result, the number of q-grams changed by the second and all following edit operations is *at most* q per operation.

Theorem 5.1   Count Filter. *[Gravano et al., 2001, Sutinen and Tarhio, 1996] Consider two strings s_1 and s_2 with the q-gram profiles $X^q(s_1)$ and $X^q(s_2)$, respectively. If s_1 and s_2 are within edit distance k, then the cardinality of the q-gram profile intersection is at least*

$$|X^q(s_1) \cap X^q(s_2)| \geq \max(|X^q(s_1)|, |X^q(s_2)|) - kq \qquad (5.5)$$

Proof. By induction. For $k = 1$ the assertion is true due to Eq. 5.4. If Eq. (5.5) is true for k, then it is also true for $k + 1$ since an additional edit operation changes at most q q-grams. □

5.3.3   POSITIONAL COUNT FILTER

The positional count filter is based on the observation that q-grams far from each other in the position of the two strings need not to be counted for the intersection, thus tightening the bound. To this end, *positional q-grams* are defined. A positional q-gram of a string s_1 is a pair $(i, gram)$, where i is the position of the first character of the q-gram $gram$ in the extended string $\#^{q-1} s_1 \#^{q-1}$. For example, the positional q-grams of the string $s_1 = \texttt{peter}$ are

$$X^P(s_1) = \{(1, \texttt{\#\#p}), (2, \texttt{\#pe}), (3, \texttt{pet}), (4, \texttt{ete}), (5, \texttt{ter}), (6, \texttt{er\#}), (7, \texttt{r\#\#})\}$$

The edit distance between two strings s_1 and s_2 is defined based on the minimum cost sequence of edit operations that transform s_1 to s_2. When a minimum edit script is applied to s_1, each character c that is inserted or deleted, shifts all characters to the right of c by one position. Also the q-grams formed by these characters are shifted and change their position. A positional q-gram (i, G_1) of s_1 is defined to *correspond* to (j, G_2) in s_2 if $G_1 = G_2$ and the characters of G_1 have been shifted by $|i - j|$ positions by the edit script. Intuitively, G_1 becomes G_2 during the execution of the edit script. This leads to the following observation.

Theorem 5.2   *[Gravano et al., 2001, Sutinen and Tarhio, 1995] If strings s_1 and s_2 are within an edit distance of k, then a positional q-gram in one cannot correspond to a positional q-gram in the other that differs from it by more than k positions.*

In the count filter we only need to count corresponding q-grams, i.e., for a given threshold k all positional q-grams with positions i and j such that $|i - j| > k$ are removed from the intersection. The number of remaining q-grams must be at least $\max(|X^P(s_1)|, |X^P(s_2)|) - kq$, otherwise the string pair (s_1, s_2) is not within edit distance k.

5.3.4   USING STRING FILTERS IN A RELATIONAL DATABASE

We discuss the application of length, count, and position filter on joins in a relational database [Gravano et al., 2001]. We illustrate the join queries on the tables in Figure 5.2, which store names of persons and an identifier for each person (the subscript annotates a name with its length for illustration purposes and is not part of the table). Although both tables include the same people, the names are spelled differently. Therefore, an equi-join on the *name* attribute (see Figure 5.3(a)) will give an empty result. If we allow an edit distance of $k = 3$ between names, all pairs of names are matched correctly (see Figures 5.3(b) and 5.3(c)).

A		B	
ID	name	ID	name
1023	Frodo Baggins$_{13}$	948483	John R. R. Tolkien$_{18}$
21	J. R. R. Tolkien$_{16}$	153494	C. S. Lewis$_{11}$
239	C.S. Lewis$_{10}$	494392	Fordo Baggins$_{13}$
863	Bilbo Baggins$_{13}$	799294	Biblo Baggins$_{13}$

Figure 5.2: Example tables for similarity joins.

```
SELECT * FROM A,B
WHERE A.name = B.name
```

(a) Equi-join on name attribute.

```
SELECT * FROM A,B
WHERE sed(A.name, B.name) <= k
```

(b) Edit distance join on name attribute.

ID	name	ID	name
1023	Frodo Baggins	494392	Fordo Baggins
21	J. R. R. Tolkien	948483	John R. R. Tolkien
239	C.S. Lewis	153494	C. S. Lewis
863	Bilbo Baggins	799294	Biblo Baggins

(c) Result of edit distance join for $k = 3$.

Figure 5.3: SQL queries for equality and similarity join.

The problem with the join in Figure 5.3(b) is its efficiency: $|A \times B|$ edit distance computations are required, which does not scale to large tables. We apply length, count, and positional count filter and show how the number of candidates, for which the edit distance must be computed, is reduced. The SQL query that includes the length filter is shown in Figure 5.4(a). The length filter will prune the pairs (J. R. R. Tolkien, C. S. Lewis), (Frodo Baggins, John R. R. Tolkien), (C.S. Lewis, John R. R. Tolkien), and (Bilbo Baggins, John R. R. Tolkien). Only 12 edit distance computations (instead of 16) are required.

For the two count filters we need auxiliary tables that store q-grams. Gravano et al. [2001] show how q-grams are produced in SQL using the substring function. Using this q-gram query we produce the table $QA(id, pos, qgram)$ for A, which stores all positional q-grams of the names in A; similarly we produce $QB(id, pos, qgram)$. The query and part of QA are shown

```
SELECT * FROM A,B
WHERE   ABS(LENGTH(A.name)-LENGTH(B.name)) <= k AND
        sed(A.name, B.name) <= k
```

(a) Length filter.

```
1     SELECT    A.id, B.id, A.name, B.name
2     FROM      A, QA, B, QB
3     WHERE     A.id = QA.id AND
4               B.id = QB.id AND
5               QA.qgram = QB.qgram AND
6               ABS(LENGTH(A.name)-LENGTH(B.name)) <= k AND
7               ABS(QA.pos-QB.pos)<=k
8     GROUP BY  A.id, B.id, A.name, B.name
9     HAVING    COUNT(*) >= LENGTH(A.name)-1-(k-1)*q AND
10              COUNT(*) >= LENGTH(B.name)-1-(k-1)*q AND
11              sed(A.name,B.name) <= k
```

(b) Count, positional, and length filters.

Figure 5.4: Similarity join with filters.

in Figure 5.5. The q-gram query requires an auxiliary table $N(i)$ that stores at least the integers $1 \leq i \leq n + q - 1$, where n is the length of the longest string in table A. The join produces a pair (s, i) for each string s and each integer from 1 to $|s| + q - 1$. The integers are used in the SELECT clause to determine the start position of the q-gram. The function SUBSTRING(s, a, b) returns the substring $s[a \ldots a + b - 1]$. It is applied to produce q-grams and to extend the string with $q - 1$ dummy characters (#). We store the q-grams in lowercase to make the join case insensitive.

The join query with count and positional filter is shown in Figure 5.4(b). The q-gram tables QA and QB are joined on the q-grams, which produces for each pair $(QA.id, QB.id)$ as many tuples as there are q-grams in the intersection between the respective q-gram profiles. The length filter is implemented in line 6. Line 7 implements the positional filter by not joining q-grams that are too far from each other. The join result is grouped by name pairs and the number of common q-grams for each name pair must pass the count filter. Only if all conditions are satisfied, a name pair is part of the candidate set and the edit distance is computed. In our example tables in Figure 5.2, only 6 (out of 16) tuples pass the filters and require an edit distance computation; the false positives are (Bilbo Baggins, Fordo Baggins) and (Frodo Baggins, Biblo Baggins), which differ only in the first four characters such that only four q-grams are affected.

As observed by Gravano et al. [2003], the query in Figure 5.5 applies the count filter only to pairs of strings that have at least one q-gram in common. The other string pairs are not part of the join result and are removed before the grouping. There might, however, be string pairs

```
CREATE TABLE QA AS
SELECT A.id, N.i AS pos,
       SUBSTRING(CONCAT(
              SUBSTRING('#..#', 1, q - 1),
              LOWER(A.name),
              SUBSTRING('#..#', 1, q - 1)),
          N.i, q) AS qgram
FROM A, N
WHERE N.i <= LENGTH(A.name) + q - 1
```

(a) Query for computing positional q-grams.

A			QA		
id	name		id	pos	qgram
1023	Frodo Baggins		1023	1	##F
21	J. R. R. Tolkien		1023	2	#Fr
239	C.S. Lewis		...	...	
863	Bilbo Baggins		21	1	##J
			21	2	#J.
			...	...	...

(b) Example q-gram table.

Figure 5.5: Computing q-grams in SQL.

that have no q-gram in common, but satisfy the count filter condition and (potentially) the edit distance constraint. Consider the count filter condition in Theorem 5.1: $|X^q(s_1) ⩎ X^q(s_2)| \geq \max(|X^q(s_1)|, |X^q(s_2)|) - kq$. For a pair of strings, (s_1, s_2), with $|X^q(s_1) ⩎ X^q(s_2)| = 0$ the count filter condition is

$$kq \geq \max(|X^q(s_1)|, |X^q(s_2)|).$$

Thus, pairs of short strings (relative to the edit distance threshold k and the value of q) can be candidates although they have no q-gram in common. An example is the string pair (IBM, BMW) for $q = 2$ and an edit distance constraint of 2. The q-gram profiles are $X^q(s_1) = \{$#I, IB, BM, M#$\}$ and $X^q(s_2) = \{$#B, BM, MW, W#$\}$ and the condition $kq \geq \max(|X^q(s_1)|, |X^q(s_2)|)$ holds. In fact, the string pair should be in the result set since $sed(\text{IBM}, \text{BMW}) = 2 \leq k$, but the intersection of the q-gram profiles is empty and the string pair is not a result of the query in Figure 5.5. To capture also the strings that are removed by the join, the query in Figure 5.5 is extended with the query in Figure 5.6, which treats short strings separately.

```
        . . .
12      UNION
13      SELECT   A.id, B.id, A.name, B.name
14      FROM     A, B
15      WHERE    LENGTH(A.name)+q-1 <= k*q AND
16               LENGTH(B.name)+q-1 <= k*q AND
17               ABS(LENGTH(A.name) - LENGTH(B.name)) <= k AND
18               sed(A.name,B.name) <= k
```

Figure 5.6: Treating short strings separately.

5.4   TREE DISTANCE BOUNDS

5.4.1   SIZE LOWER BOUND

Similar to the length bound in the string case, for trees a lower bound on the unit cost edit distance is given by the tree sizes. Let $|T|$ denote the number of nodes in tree T. The *size lower bound* is based on the observation that the surplus nodes in the larger tree must be deleted.

$$ted(T_1, T_2) \geq \text{abs}(|T_1| - |T_2|) \tag{5.6}$$

The size lower bound is computed in constant time (given the tree sizes). For many applications it will not be effective enough since it ignores both labels and structure of the tree.

5.4.2   INTERSECTION LOWER BOUND

A simple lower bound that accounts for the labels is based on the intersection of the node label bags of two trees.

Theorem 5.3   Intersection Lower Bound.   *Let $ted(T_1, T_2)$ denote the unit cost tree edit distance between trees T_1, T_2, let L_1 and L_2 be the bags of labels of T_1 and T_2, respectively.*

$$ted(T_1, T_2) \geq \max(|L_1|, |L_2|) - |L_1 \Cap L_2| \tag{5.7}$$

Proof. The right-hand side of Eq. (5.7) is the number of nodes in the larger tree that cannot be mapped to a node with the same label in the smaller tree. Each of these nodes either needs to be mapped to a node with a different label (incurring a rename) or the node is not mapped (incurring an insert or a delete operation). Thus, for each node an edit operation is required, leading to the lower bound.   □

The intersection lower bound may be too coarse since it completely disregards the structure of the tree. Refined lower bounds capture the structure by considering the order of the labels in tree traversals or by considering small substructures that capture the local neighborhood of the nodes.

An idea similar to the intersection lower bound is the label histogram filter [Kailing et al., 2004]. All node labels of a tree are assigned to bins of a label histogram and the Manhattan distance (cf. Section 4.2) between two histogram vectors divided by two is used as a lower bound for the tree edit distance.

5.4.3   TRAVERSAL STRING LOWER BOUND

The traversal string lower bound is based on the string edit distance. The trees are transformed to sequences of node labels by traversing their nodes in preorder or postorder. The preorder traversal visits the root node first and then traverses all subtrees rooted in the children of the root node in preorder. The postorder traversal first visits the subtrees of the children, then the root node. The sequence of node labels given by a traversal is considered as a string. Each "character" of the string is a node label. The preorder string of a tree T is denoted with $pre(T)$, the postorder string with $post(T)$, the unit cost tree edit distance is $ted(T_i, T_j)$ and the string edit distance is $sed(s_i, s_j)$.

Example 5.4   Figure 5.7 shows two tree pairs, T_1, T_2 and T_3, T_4, the respective preorder and postorder strings, and a minimum cost edit mapping. For trees T_1 and T_2, the string distances between the preorder and postorder traversals are equal to the tree edit distance. Trees T_3 and T_4 have identical preorder strings, although the trees differ. The postorder strings can distinguish the trees. The edit distance between the trees is larger than the string distances since the strings loose some of the structure information.

The observation that the string distance between the traversal strings is at most the edit distance between their trees generalizes to the lower bound theorem for traversal strings.

Theorem 5.5   Traversal String Lower Bound.   *[Guha et al., 2002] If two trees T_1 and T_2 are at unit cost edit distance k, then the string edit distance between their preorder or postorder traversal strings is at most k.*

$$ted(T_1, T_2) \geq max(sed(pre(T_1), pre(T_2)), sed(post(T_1), post(T_2)))$$

Proof. *Preorder:* Each edit operation on a tree affects at most one character in the preorder string. Figure 5.8 illustrates the insertion of a node v as the k-th child of node p; the children of p at

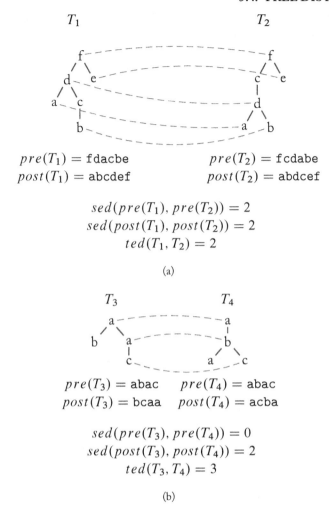

$pre(T_1) = $ fdacbe

$post(T_1) = $ abcdef

$pre(T_2) = $ fcdabe

$post(T_2) = $ abdcef

$$sed(pre(T_1), pre(T_2)) = 2$$
$$sed(post(T_1), post(T_2)) = 2$$
$$ted(T_1, T_2) = 2$$

(a)

$pre(T_3) = $ abac $pre(T_4) = $ abac

$post(T_3) = $ bcaa $post(T_4) = $ acba

$$sed(pre(T_3), pre(T_4)) = 0$$
$$sed(post(T_3), post(T_4)) = 2$$
$$ted(T_3, T_4) = 3$$

(b)

Figure 5.7: Traversal string lower bound.

positions k to m become children of the new node v. Before the insertion, the preorder traversal of the subtree rooted in p is

$$p\ pre(t_1) \ldots pre(t_{k-1})pre(t_k) \ldots pre(t_m)pre(t_{m+1}) \ldots pre(t_f).$$

After the insertion of node v the preorder string is:

$$p\ pre(t_1) \ldots pre(t_{k-1})\ v\ pre(t_k) \ldots pre(t_m)pre(t_{m+1}) \ldots pre(t_f)$$

The string distance between the two preorder strings is 1. Deletion is the reverse operation of insertion and analogous reasoning holds. The rename operation replaces a single character in the preorder string. Thus the lower bound holds for $k = 1$. We show case $k > 1$ by induction. If the lower bound holds for k edit operations, then it also holds for $k + 1$ operations since the new operation increases the distance between the preorder strings at most by one. *Postorder:* Analogous reasoning. □

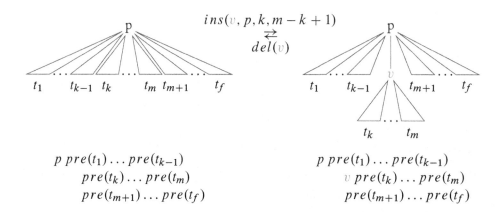

$$p\ pre(t_1)\ldots pre(t_{k-1})$$
$$pre(t_k)\ldots pre(t_m)$$
$$pre(t_{m+1})\ldots pre(t_f)$$

$$p\ pre(t_1)\ldots pre(t_{k-1})$$
$$v\ pre(t_k)\ldots pre(t_m)$$
$$pre(t_{m+1})\ldots pre(t_f)$$

Figure 5.8: Lower bound proof: insertion and preorder traversal.

5.4.4   PQ-GRAM LOWER BOUND

In this section we show that the *pq*-gram distance, which can be computed in $O(n \log n)$ time and $O(n)$ space, provides a lower bound approximation for the fanout weighted tree edit distance (cf. Section 3.2.1). The lower bound guarantee allows us to safely use *pq*-grams for pruning, for example, in a distance join. With the lower bound guarantee the pruning produces no false negatives, i.e., the pruning increases the efficiency without changing the join result.

The lower bound proof [Augsten et al., 2010b] proceeds in three steps:

1. *Unchanged pq-grams:* Assume trees, T_1 and T_2, with indexes $X_\lambda^{pq}(T_1)$ and $X_\lambda^{pq}(T_2)$, respectively, an edit mapping, $M \subseteq N_\epsilon(T) \times N_\epsilon(T_2)$, and the inverse edit mapping, M^{-1}, of M. We define the unchanged *pq*-grams of T_1, $U(T_1, M, T_2)$, and show

$$|X_\lambda^{pq}(T_1) \uplus X_\lambda^{pq}(T_2)| \geq |U(T_1, M, T_2)| = |U(T_2, M^{-1}, T_1)|.$$

2. *Upper Bound for the pq-gram Distance:* Using the above result, we prove the following upper bound for the *pq*-gram distance, where $D(M)$, $I(M)$, and $R(M)$ partition the mapping

M into deletions, insertions, and renames, respectively:

$$\begin{aligned}
D^{pq}(T_1, T_2) &= |X^{pq}_\lambda(T_1)| + |X^{pq}_\lambda(T_2)| - 2|X^{pq}_\lambda(T_1) \cap X^{pq}_\lambda(T_2)| \\
&\leq \sum_{(v,v') \in D(M)} \max(2q + 2, 2f_v + 4q - 2) + \\
&\quad \sum_{(v,v') \in I(M)} \max(2q + 2, 2f_{v'} + 4q - 2) + \\
&\quad \sum_{(v,v') \in R(M)} \max(2q + 2, f_v + f_{v'} + 4q - 2)
\end{aligned}$$

3. *Lower Bound for the Tree Edit Distance:* Finally we show that the upper bound for the *pq*-gram distance (divided by 2) is a lower bound for the fanout weighted tree edit distance and conclude:

$$\frac{D^{pq}(T_1, T_2)}{2} \leq \text{ted}_{fout}(T_1, T_2)$$

The lower bound holds for the minimal *pq*-gram pattern ($p = 1$). For larger patterns ($p > 1$) the *pq*-gram distance is more sensitive to structure changes than the fanout weighted tree edit distance and can grow beyond the fanout weighted tree edit distance.

The *pq*-gram distance also provides a lower bound for normalized tree edit distances: $D^{pq}(T_1, T_2)/2x \leq \text{ted}_{fout}(T_1, T_2)/x$. Note though that not all normalizations yield a pseudo-metric. The pseudo-metric properties hold for the normalization of Definition 4.12, which normalizes the pq-gram distance to values between 0 and 1.

Step 1: Unchanged pq-Grams

Definition 5.6   Unchanged pq-Grams.   Let T_1 and T_2 be two trees, $M \subseteq N_\epsilon(T_1) \times N_\epsilon(T_2)$ be an edit mapping, and $X^{pq}(T_2)$ be the set of all *pq*-grams of T_2. A *pq*-gram G_1 of T_1 is *unchanged* iff there is a *pq*-gram G_2 of T_2 such that M maps all non-dummy nodes of G_1 to nodes of G_2 with the same label, and vice versa. The set of all unchanged *pq*-grams of T_1 is denoted as $U(T_1, M, T_2)$:

$$\begin{aligned}
G_1 \in U(T_1, M, T_2) \Leftrightarrow &\exists\, G_2 \in X^{pq}(T_2) : \\
&\forall v \in N(G_1) \cap N(T_1)\, \exists v' \in N(G_2)[(v, v') \in M \wedge \lambda(v) = \lambda(v')] \wedge \\
&\forall v' \in N(G_2) \cap N(T_2)\, \exists v \in N(G_1)[(v, v') \in M \wedge \lambda(v) = \lambda(v')]
\end{aligned}$$

For each unchanged *pq*-gram of one tree there is at least one *pq*-gram in the other tree with the same label tuple. Therefore the cardinality of the index intersection of two trees is at least the cardinality of the unchanged *pq*-grams.

Lemma 5.7   *Given an edit mapping M between the nodes of two trees, T_1 and T_2, the respective pq-gram indexes, $X^{pq}_\lambda(T_1)$ and $X^{pq}_\lambda(T_2)$, and the inverse mapping $M^{-1} = \{(v', v) \mid (v, v') \in M\}$, then*

$$|X^{pq}_\lambda(T_1) \cap X^{pq}_\lambda(T_2)| \geq |U(T_1, M, T_2)| = |U(T_2, M^{-1}, T_1)|. \tag{5.8}$$

Step 2: Upper Bound for the pq-Gram Distance

The upper bound for the pq-gram distance is a function of the deletions, insertions, and renames defined by M. Intuitively, we count the non-matching pq-grams between two trees, T_1 and T_2, to derive an upper bound for their pq-gram distance.

Lemma 5.8 *Let M be an edit mapping between two trees, T_1 and T_2, $D(M) = \{(v, \epsilon) \mid (v, \epsilon) \in M\}$ the deletions, $I(M) = \{(\epsilon, v') \mid (\epsilon, v') \in M\}$ the insertions, and $R(M) = \{(v, v') \mid (v, v') \in M \land \lambda(v) \neq \lambda(v') \land v \neq \epsilon \land v' \neq \epsilon\}$ the renames, $p = 1, q > 0$, then*

$$\begin{aligned}
D^{pq}(T_1, T_2) \leq \ & \textstyle\sum_{(v,v') \in D(M)} \max(2q + 2, 2f_v + 4q - 2) + \\
& \textstyle\sum_{(v,v') \in I(M)} \max(2q + 2, 2f_{v'} + 4q - 2) + \\
& \textstyle\sum_{(v,v') \in R(M)} \max(2q + 2, f_v + f_{v'} + 4q - 2).
\end{aligned} \tag{5.9}$$

Step 3: Lower Bound for the Tree Edit Distance

Theorem 5.9 Lower Bound. *Let $p = 1$ and $k \geq \max(2q - 1, 2)$ be the cost of aligning leaf nodes. The pq-gram distance provides a lower bound for the fanout weighted tree edit distance, i.e., for any two trees, T_1 and T_2,*

$$\frac{D^{pq}(T_1, T_2)}{2} \leq \text{ted}_{fout}(T_1, T_2).$$

5.4.5 BINARY BRANCH LOWER BOUND

Binary branches [Yang et al., 2005], which were discussed in Section 4.4.1, provide a lower bound for the unit cost edit distance. A transformation of the input tree to a binary tree is used to produce the binary branch tokens. In a binary tree, a node can have a *left* and a *right* outgoing edge. The binary tree transformation is done in two steps:

1. link all neighboring siblings in a tree with edges; and

2. delete all parent-child edges except the edge to the first child.

Example 5.10 Figure 5.9 illustrates the transformation of a tree T_1 to the binary tree T_2. The left edges in the binary tree (solid lines) represent parent-child relationships in the original tree, the right edges (dashed lines) represent right sibling relationships.

The binary branches of a tree T_1 are produced as follows: (a) transform T_1 into a binary tree T_2, (b) extend the binary tree T_2 with dummy nodes ϵ such that the resulting tree T_2^{bb} is a full

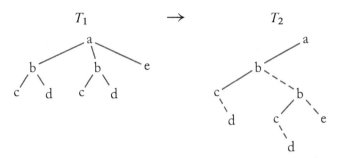

Figure 5.9: Binary tree transformation.

binary tree, all leaf nodes are dummy nodes, and all non-leaves are nodes of the original tree T_1, (c) each subtree of T_2^{bb} that consists of a node and two children is a *binary branch*.

Example 5.11   Figure 5.10 shows the extension of the binary tree T_2 with dummy nodes ϵ and the binary branches that are produced for the extended tree T_2^{bb}. In the original tree T_1 (cf. Figure 5.9), a binary branch consists of a node, its first child (or a dummy node), and its right sibling (or a dummy node).

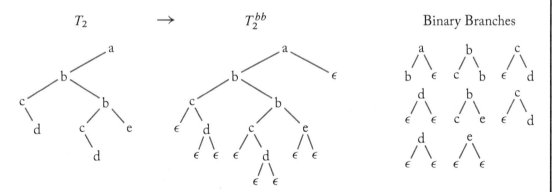

Figure 5.10: Extended binary tree and binary branches.

The binary branches of a tree are serialized into label triples (p, c_1, c_2) where p is the label of the parent node, c_1 the label of the left child, and c_2 the label of the right child of p. While the binary branches are unique subtrees of T_2^{bb}, their label triples can be duplicated. For example, the triple (c, ϵ, d) appears twice for the tree in Figure 5.10. Henceforth we will refer to both the binary branches and their label triples as binary branches if the distinction is clear from the context.

Definition 5.12   Binary Branch Distance.   Given two trees T_1 and T_2 with their bags of binary branches $X_\lambda^{bb}(T_1)$ and $X_\lambda^{bb}(T_2)$, respectively, the binary branch distance between T_1 and T_2 is defined as

$$D^{bb}(T_1, T_2) = |X_\lambda^{bb}(T_1)| + |X_\lambda^{bb}(T_2)| - 2|X_\lambda^{bb}(T_1) \Cap X_\lambda^{bb}(T_2)|$$

Theorem 5.13   Binary Branch Lower Bound.   *[Yang et al., 2005] Let T_1 and T_2 be two trees, $ted(T_1, T_2)$ the unit cost tree edit between the trees, and $D^{bb}(T_1, T_2)$ the binary branch distance, we have*

$$ted(T_1, T_2) \geq \frac{D^{bb}(T_1, T_2)}{5}$$

Proof. The proof is based on the observation that a single edit operation in the original tree increases the binary branch distance by at most 5. The binary branch distance is increased by each binary branch in T_1 or T_2 that does not have a match in the binary branches of the other tree. We sketch the proof here; the full proof can be found in [Yang et al., 2005]. The *rename* operation does not change the structure of the tree. The renamed node is part of two binary branches in each tree, thus overall four binary branches are affected (cf. Figure 5.11(a)). The *insert* operation changes the structure of the tree. Since a binary branch consists of a node, its first child, and its right sibling, structure changes that modify these relationships affect binary branches. When a new node x is inserted to transform T_1 into T_2, then two binary branches are affected in T_1 and three binary branches are affected in T_2 (cf. Figure 5.11(b)).   □

5.4.6   CONSTRAINED EDIT DISTANCE UPPER BOUND

The constrained edit distance was introduced in Section 3.2.3. With respect to the standard tree edit distance, the edit mapping between the nodes is restricted by an additional constraint. The restriction reduces the search space for the minimum cost edit mapping and algorithms with $O(n^2)$ asymptotic runtime in the number n of tree nodes have been proposed to solve the constrained edit distance problem [Zhang, 1995]. This is faster than the standard tree edit distance, which requires $O(n^3)$ time in the worst case. The constrained edit distance is an upper bound of the tree edit distance.

Theorem 5.14   Constrained Edit Distance Upper Bound.   *[Guha et al., 2002] Given two trees T_1 and T_2, the constrained edit distance $cted(T_1, T_2)$, and the unconstrained edit distance $ted(T_1, T_2)$*

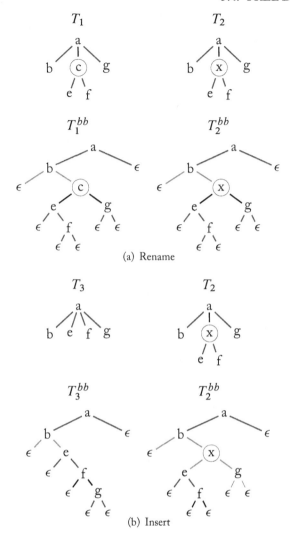

Figure 5.11: Binary branches affected by edit operations.

between T_1 and T_2, we have

$$cted(T_1, T_2) \geq ted(T_1, T_2)$$

Proof. Assume $cted(T_1, T_2) < ted(T_1, T_2)$. Then there is a constrained edit mapping M_c with cost $c(M_c) = cted(T_1, T_2)$ and an unconstrained edit mapping M with cost $c(M) =$

$ted(T_1, T_2)$. Since M_c is (by definition) also an unconstrained edit mapping, the cost of M is not minimal, which contradicts $c(M) = ted(T_1, T_2)$. □

5.5 FURTHER READINGS

String Similarity Queries A large body of work deals with answering similarity queries with edit distance constraints efficiently. The techniques presented in this section are based on q-grams [Gravano et al., 2001, Li et al., 2008]. Xiao et al. [2008a] present a filter technique that also takes into account the non-matching q-grams. Variable length q-grams have been presented by Li et al. [2007] and Yang et al. [2008]. Other approaches are based on B^+-trees [Zhang et al., 2010] (B^{ed}-tree), tries [Chaudhuri and Kaushik, 2009, Fenz et al., 2012, Ji et al., 2009, Li et al., 2009, Wang et al., 2010], string enumeration [Arasu et al., 2006] (PartEnum), string partitioning [Li et al., 2011, Wang et al., 2011, 2009], or asymmetric signatures [Qin et al., 2011]. Hadjielteheriou and Srivastava [2011] provide an extensive survey of techniques for string similarity queries.

Metric Techniques A number of techniques have been developed for similarity functions that are metrics or pseudo-metrics. These techniques use the triangle inequality to derive upper and lower bounds. Assume, for example, the threshold $\tau = 3$ and the string edit distances $sed(s_1, s_2) = 1$, $sed(s_2, z) = 1$ that have already been computed. Then, for the distance $sed(s_1, z)$ the following bounds are derived using the triangle inequality:

$$|sed(s_1, s_2) - sed(s_2, z)| \leq sed(s_1, z) \leq sed(s_1, s_2) + sed(s_2, z)$$

Due to the upper bound $sed(s_1, s_2) + sed(s_2, z) = 2$ the distance between s_1 and z needs not be computed.

A large number of techniques have been proposed for search and join queries in metric space [Samet, 2005, Zezula et al., 2006]. A well-known index structure for metric spaces is the M-tree [Ciaccia et al., 1997], which uses the triangle inequality to prune branches of the index tree. Guha et al. [2002] combine the traversal string lower bound and the constrained edit distance upper bound for trees with metric techniques in order to join XML documents. Silva et al. [2013b] propose a physical join operator for metric predicates in relational databases. The conceptual evaluation and query transformation rules for various types of similarity queries based on metric distances, e.g., similarity group and similarity join, have been studied by Silva et al. [2013a].

CHAPTER 6

Filters for Token Equality Joins

In this chapter we consider joins between two relations R and S with attributes $(id, toks)$, where id is an identifier of some object (for example, a string) and $toks$ is the set of tokens for the object identified by id (for example, the q-grams of a string). The join predicate is an overlap constraint on the $toks$ attribute, which represents the similarity between objects. For example, find all pairs of objects which have at least 10 tokens in common.

This kind of join, also known as *set similarity join*, requires computing intersections between pairs of token sets and returns only the pairs that meet the overlap constraint. The straightforward strategy for evaluating it is a nested-loop join that computes n^2 intersections for two relations with n tuples each. This is very slow when n grows large. Fortunately, there are better strategies to compute this join. In this chapter we discuss techniques to improve the efficiency of the set similarity join. Efficient strategies are based on the following core observations:

- empty and very small intersections need not be computed; and

- some pairs of token sets can be pruned by inspecting only a small subsets of the tokens.

6.1 TOKEN EQUALITY JOIN – AVOIDING EMPTY INTERSECTIONS

An empty intersection between token sets indicates zero similarity between the corresponding objects. The similarity threshold in joins is always larger than zero, otherwise the join predicate would be true for all pairs resulting in a cross product of the input tables. Pairs of objects with an empty intersection on their token sets will never be in the join result.

In the nested-loop approach, all intersections are computed, including the empty intersections. Since the join result is typically much smaller than the cross product, most intersections will not satisfy the join threshold. The goal is to avoid the computation of empty intersections altogether.

Consider the join between the tables R and S in Figure 6.1. The nested-loop join computes 9 intersections, but only 3 intersections (highlighted) are non-empty. While one can think of techniques to detect empty intersection early in the process of computing the intersection of a pair of sets, the number of such computations remains quadratic and such an approach will not scale to a large number of tuples.

	R		S	
id	$toks$	id	$toks$	
r_1	$\{a,b\}$	s_1	$\{a,b\}$	
r_2	$\{a,c\}$	s_2	$\{f,g\}$	
r_3	$\{d,e\}$	s_3	$\{c,h\}$	

Intersections computed by the nested-loop approach:

$$\mathbf{r_1 \cap s_1 = 2} \quad r_1 \cap s_2 = 0 \quad r_1 \cap s_3 = 0$$
$$\mathbf{r_2 \cap s_1 = 1} \quad r_2 \cap s_2 = 0 \quad \mathbf{r_2 \cap s_3 = 1}$$
$$r_3 \cap s_1 = 0 \quad r_3 \cap s_2 = 0 \quad r_3 \cap s_3 = 0$$

Figure 6.1: Set-based nested-loop join also computes empty intersections.

Token Equality Joins for Sets   The solution to the problem is to break up the sets and express the set similarity join as an equality join on tokens, called *token equality join*. Equality joins have a long tradition in databases and efficient techniques to evaluate similarity joins have been developed, for example, hash joins and sort-merge joins. The algorithm works as follows (c.f. Figure 6.2):

1. *Unnest:* Produce a new table $IR(idr, tok)$, which contains a tuple for each element of each token set of R. A tuple consists of an object identifier idr and one token tok of the respective token set in R. Similarly, the table $IS(ids, tok)$ is computed for S.

2. *Join:* Compute the equality join $IR \bowtie IS$ on tokens, which produces a tuple (idr, ids, tok) for every token that idr and ids have in common.

3. *Group:* Partition the join result into groups of tuples with identical values in idr and ids. The number of tuples in each group is the intersection between the respective token sets idr and ids.

   Unnesting the token sets requires a single scan over the relations R and S. The join is computed using an efficient hash or sort-merge join, which avoids comparing all pairs of tuples. The sort-merge join, for example, sorts both relations and merges the sorted relations by scanning them in a synchronized fashion. Note that the join result only contains pairs of token sets with a non-empty intersection. The grouping step can be computed efficiently by sorting or hashing.
   The approach will not give a correct result for duplicate tokens, i.e., for token bags. Consider, for example, two tuples $(r_4, \{a,a\}) \in R$ and $(s_4, \{a,a\}) \in S$. Then Step 2 of the token equality join (cf. Figure 6.2) produces four tuples (r_4, s_4, a) and Step 3 produces a tuple $(r_4, s_4, 4)$. This is wrong since the intersection between the token sets r_4 and s_4 is 2, not 4.

Token Equality Joins for Bags   In order to deal with duplicate tokens, the token bags must either be converted to sets using the counting or the frequency approach (cf. Section 4.1). When the counting approach is used, the token equality join for sets is applied to the token-counter pairs.

Step 1: Unnest

IR		IS	
idr	tok	ids	tok
r_1	a	s_1	a
r_1	b	s_1	b
r_2	a	s_2	f
r_2	c	s_2	g
r_3	d	s_3	c
r_3	e	s_3	h

Step 2: Join

$IR \bowtie IS$		
idr	ids	tok
r_1	s_1	a
r_1	s_1	b
r_2	s_1	a
r_2	s_3	c

Step 3: Group

$\gamma_{idr,ids;\text{COUNT}(*)}(IR \bowtie IS)$		
idr	ids	$\text{COUNT}(*)$
r_1	s_1	2
r_2	s_1	1
r_2	s_3	1

Figure 6.2: Token equality join does not compute empty intersections.

An example of tokens stored using the frequency approach is the pq-gram index in Figure 4.18. The frequency approach requires slightly different queries. Algorithm 9 computes the token equality join between two token tables $X_1(id_1, tok, freq_1)$ and $X_2(id_2, tok, freq_2)$; each tuple stores a token tok of object $id_{1/2}$ that appears $freq_{1/2}$ times in the token bag of $id_{1/2}$. The algorithm returns all pairs (id_1, id_2) such that the Jaccard distance between the respective token sets is within the threshold τ. For the Jaccard distance the sizes of the token bags are required, which are computed in the first two lines of the algorithm and are stored in the tables PS_1 and PS_2.

Algorithm 9: BagTokenEqJoin(X_1, X_2, τ)

---

1 $PS_1 \leftarrow \gamma_{id_1;\text{SUM}(freq_1) \rightarrow size_1}(X_1)$;

2 $PS_2 \leftarrow \gamma_{id_2;\text{SUM}(freq_2) \rightarrow size_2}(X_2)$;

3 $A \leftarrow X_1 \bowtie X_2$;

4 $B \leftarrow \gamma_{id_1,id_2;\text{SUM}(\min(freq_1, freq_2)) \rightarrow overlap}(A)$;

5 $C \leftarrow B \bowtie PS_1 \bowtie PS_2$;

6 $D \leftarrow \pi_{id_1,id_2}(\sigma_{1 - \frac{overlap}{size_1 + size_2 - overlap} \leq \tau}(C))$;

7 **return** D;

Example 6.1   Figure 6.3 illustrates Algorithm 9 and shows the windowed pq-gram join ($w = 3$, $p = q = 2$) between two sets of example trees, F_1 and F_2. To increase the readability, the node labels of the windowed pq-grams are shown instead of their hash values (cf. Section 4.5.5). The inputs to the algorithm are the windowed pq-gram indexes, X_1 and X_2, of the two forests, F_1 and F_2, respectively. First, the tables PS_1 and PS_2 are computed as shown in the figure. Then the indexes are joined (Table A). Next, the intersection of the pq-gram indexes is computed (Table B) unless the intersection is empty. An element that appears n times in bag B_1 and m times in bag B_2 appears $\min(n, m)$ times in the intersection $B_1 \sqcap B_2$. The intersection result is extended with the size of the pq-gram profiles (Table C). Finally, all pairs of trees within windowed pq-gram distance $\tau = 0.5$ are selected (Table D).

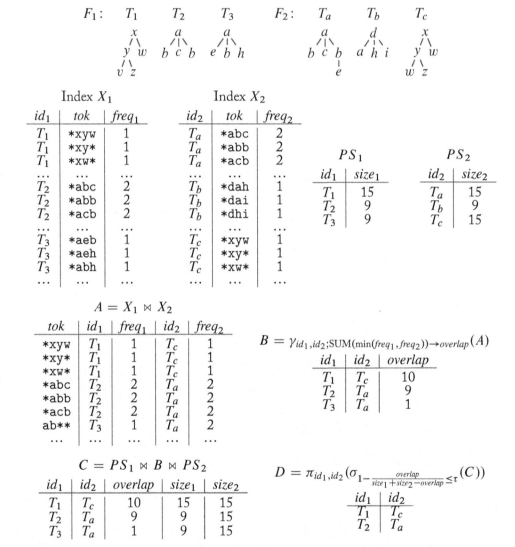

Figure 6.3: Token equality join on tree sets F_1 and F_2 using windowed pq-grams.

The token equality join exploits the dissimilarity between the token sets and works best when many token sets are dissimilar and have no common tokens. The efficiency of this approach is undermined by frequent tokens that appear in almost all token sets (also known as "stop words") resulting in a large intermediate join result. This issue is addressed by the so-called prefix filter discussed in the next section.

6.2   PREFIX FILTER – AVOIDING SMALL INTERSECTIONS

Prefix filtering [Chaudhuri et al., 2006] is based on the observation that the overlap between two sets cannot reach a given threshold if a specific subset (called *prefix*) of the two sets has an empty intersection. Thus, the computation of the intersection between two sets cannot only be avoided when their intersection is zero (as discussed in the previous section), but also when the intersection of their prefixes is zero.

The prefix of length k of a set is the subset of its first k elements in sort order. The sort order need not be alphanumeric, but can be any strict total order defined on the tokens. We define the prefix filter principle for overlap constraints and for Jaccard constraints. We denote overlap thresholds with t, where $t > 0$ is an integer, and Jaccard thresholds with τ, where $\tau \in (0, 1]$ is a real number.

6.2.1   PREFIX FILTER FOR OVERLAP SIMILARITY

For the overlap similarity, the prefix filter principle is as follows.

Theorem 6.2   Prefix Filtering Principle.   *Given two sets A and B, a strict total order defined on the elements of both sets, and an integer threshold t, if $|A \cap B| \geq t$, then the $(|A| - t + 1)$-prefix A_p of A and the $(|B| - t + 1)$-prefix B_p of B with respect to the given order share at least one element, $A_p \cap B_p \neq \emptyset$.*

Proof. We call $A_s = A \setminus A_p$, $|A_s| = t - 1$, the suffix of A and $B_s = B \setminus B_p$, $|B_s| = t - 1$, the suffix of B. Proof by contradiction. Assume $|A \cap B| \geq t$ and $A_p \cap B_p = \emptyset$. Due to $A_p \cap B_p = \emptyset$ the last (in sort order) element a of A_p is either larger or smaller than the last (in sort order) element b of B_p. If $a < b$, then $a < x$ for all elements x of the suffix B_s, thus $A_p \cap B_s = \emptyset$, i.e., A_p does not overlap with B and $A_s \cap B = A \cap B$. Since $|A_s| = t - 1$, $|A_s \cap B| = |A \cap B| \leq t - 1$, which contradicts the assumption $|A \cap B| \geq t$. Symmetric reasoning holds for $b < a$.   □

Example 6.3   Consider the token sets $A = \{a, c, f, g, m\}$, $B = \{b, c, f, g, m, p\}$, $C = \{a, h, g, m, p\}$, and the overlap threshold $t = 4$. The prefix lengths are $|A| - t + 1 = |C| - t + 1 = 2$ for A resp. C and $|B| - t + 1 = 3$ for B. Figure 6.4 shows the sorted arrays (alphabetical order) and the prefixes shaded in gray. We want to find all pairs of sets with overlap of at least 4 and use the prefix filter to prune pairs of sets that cannot reach the threshold.

The prefix of A has elements common with the prefixes of both B and C, thus (A, B) and (A, C) are candidate pairs. The prefix of B has no common element with the prefix of C and we conclude $|B \cap C| < 4$ using the prefix filtering principle (in fact, $|B \cap C| = 3$). Note that the prefix filter condition is necessary but not sufficient, i.e., the filter may produce false positives. The computation of the intersection for the candidate pairs results in $|A \cap B| = 4$ and $|A \cap C| = 3$. The pair (A, C) is a false positive.

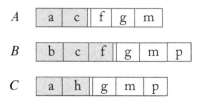

Figure 6.4: Prefix filtering.

The result of the prefix filtering is a set of candidate pairs. The prefix filter guarantees that all pairs (A, B) that satisfy the similarity threshold ($|A \cap B| \geq t$) are in the candidate set, i.e., there are no false negatives. Since the prefix filter produces false positives, for each candidate pair the overlap $|A \cap B|$ must be computed to verify if the similarity threshold is in fact reached.

The goal is to produce as few candidates as possible. Whenever two sets have a common token in the prefix, they must be in the candidate set. The prefix filter is more effective if the prefixes contain infrequent tokens with few matches in other prefixes. Since the order of the tokens can be freely chosen (as long as the same order is applied to all sets), infrequent tokens should be before frequent tokens in the sort order. A common approach [Chaudhuri et al., 2006] is to sort tokens in ascending order by their document frequency. The document frequency of a token is the number of token sets in the relation in which the token appears.

The document frequency ordering requires a precomputation step to compute the document frequencies of all tokens. For a relation $IR(id, tok)$ the document frequency df is computed as $O(tok, df) \leftarrow \gamma_{tok;\text{COUNT}(*)}(IR)$ by grouping on tokens and counting the number of tokens in each group. The resulting relation $O(tok, df)$ is then joined with IR to assign the document frequency to each token. To produce the prefixes, the tokens are grouped by id and sorted by their document frequency.

In a join scenario, both relations must follow the same token order. Since the join partner of a relation is not known upfront, the order also cannot be precomputed. Further, the document frequency should consider the frequency of a token in *both* relations. To allow at least some precomputation, a heuristics that combines the document frequencies of two relations can be applied. Xiao et al. [2008b] use the product of the document frequencies of the two relations.

Overall, the prefix approach for two relations $R(id, toks)$ and $S(id, toks)$ and an integer overlap threshold t involves the following steps:

1. *Unnest:* Compute the relations $IR(id, tok)$ and $IS(id, tok)$ from R and S, respectively, as is done in Step 1 of the token equality join.

2. *Compute Prefixes:* For each token set *toks* in R compute its prefix, i.e., the subset of the first $|toks| - t + 1$ tokens in a global token order O. Produce a table $PR(idr, ptok)$ that contains a tuple for each token in the prefix of each token set. Similarly, compute $PS(ids, ptok)$ for relation S.

3. *Join Prefixes:* Join PR and PS on the (prefix) tokens and keep pairs of token sets with at least one common token as candidates, $C(idr, ids) \leftarrow \pi_{ids, idr}(PR \bowtie PS)$.

4. *Verify Candidates:* For each pair in the candidate set the intersection must be computed to remove false positives. Since only the token identifiers are known, an additional join with the token set tables is required, i.e., $IR \bowtie C \bowtie IS$, resulting in tuples of the form (idr, ids, tok). On this result, the group/count of the token equality join (Step 3) is applied to compute the final result.

6.2.2   PREFIX FILTER FOR JACCARD SIMILARITY

So far we have considered a threshold on the overlap. The prefix filter also works for thresholds on the Jaccard similarity, $J(X, Y) = \frac{|X \cap Y|}{|X \cup Y|} \geq \tau$. In this case, the prefix length of X is $|X| - \lceil \tau |X| \rceil + 1$ and the prefix length of Y is $|Y| - \lceil \tau |Y| \rceil + 1$.

The prefix length of Y can be further reduced if $|X| \geq |Y|$. In this case, a prefix length of $|Y| - \lceil \frac{2\tau}{1+\tau} |Y| \rceil + 1$ is enough to guarantee that an empty intersection of the prefixes implies $J(X, Y) < \tau$, i.e., the pair (X, Y) can be pruned safely. This is used by Xiao et al. [2011] for self joins, where the two joined tables are identical. The Jaccard similarity is symmetric, i.e., $J(X, Y) = J(Y, X)$. Therefore, in a self join $R \bowtie_{J(R.toks, S.toks) \geq \tau} R$, each pair needs to be considered only in one direction. Further, token sets with identical id values need not be considered and can be added to the result as a final step since $J(X, X) = 1$. Overall, instead of $|R|^2$ only $R(R - 1)/2$ similarities are computed.

The efficiency for self joins can be improved by substituting Steps 2 and 3 in the algorithm for prefix joins (cf. Section 6.2.1) by the following steps.

2. *Compute Prefixes:* For each token set X in R compute its prefix of length $|X| - \lceil \tau |X| \rceil + 1$ and produce a table $PR(idr, tokr, lenr)$ that contains a tuple for each token $tokr$ in the prefix and stores the size of the token set $lenr = |X|$. Similarly, compute a table $PS(ids, toks, lens)$ for the prefixes of length $|X| - \lceil \frac{2\tau}{1+\tau} |X| \rceil + 1$ of each token set X in R.

3. *Join Prefixes:* Join PR and PS on the (prefix) tokens and keep pairs of token sets with at least one common token as candidates, $C(idr, ids) \leftarrow \pi_{ids, idr}(PR \bowtie_{tokr = toks \wedge lenr \geq lens} PS)$.

We store the length of each token set in the prefix tables PR and PS. PR stores the full prefix, called *probing prefix*, PS only stores the short prefix, called *indexing prefix*. In the join we only consider pairs that satisfy the condition $|X| \geq |Y|$ such that we can use the probing prefix for X and the indexing prefix for Y. In this join, we compare both (X, Y) and (Y, X)

if $|X| = |Y|$, which is not necessary. This can be avoided by giving each tuple a new identifier id_len such that id_len for X is smaller than id_len for X' if $|X| < |X'|$. Then we can use $tokr = toks \wedge PR.id\_len > PS.id\_len$ as a join predicate in Step 3.

This approach for self joins reduces the candidate set since one of the prefixes is shorter. It can be extended to joins between two different tables R and S by computing the self join for $R \cup S$ and removing the pairs that originate from the same table [Xiao et al., 2011].

Both the token equality join and the prefix filter break the boundaries of the sets and rephrase the set similarity join as an equality join over tokens. When the sets are sufficiently different, these approaches can break the quadratic complexity of the nested-loop join. The nested-loop join must compute the intersection for all pairs of sets. The equality join approaches need not consider pairs with an empty resp. too small an overlap. This feature leads to major performance improvements and sets them apart from other methods that merely improve the efficiency of the overlap computation.

6.2.3   EFFECTIVENESS OF PREFIX FILTERING

We showcase the effectiveness of the prefix filter on a real world dataset. We pick a subset of the records in the DBLP[1] bibliography consisting of the publications in major database venues,[2] resulting in 12k records. The records have schema $(pid, title, venue)$, where pid is an integer key. We create a q-gram token index ($q = 5$) for the title attribute, $I(pid, tk, len)$, where tk is the token and len is the length of the tokenized title (avg. 59.2). Further, we create prefix indexes for the Jaccard thresholds $\tau \in \{0.95, 0.9, 0.8, 0.7, 0.6\}$; the tokens are ordered by increasing document frequency.

We compute a similarity self join on the title strings using the prefix filter approach. The prefix indexes are joined on tokens to produce candidate pairs of publications. Table 6.1 shows the number of candidates for the different thresholds and the size of the final result.

Threshold τ	#(Candidates)	#(Result tuples)
0.60	1,987,763	12,867
0.70	872,531	12,565
0.80	298,743	12,393
0.90	63,319	12,289
0.95	24,067	12,233

Table 6.1: Number of candidates produced by prefix filter.

The prefix filter join is not faster than the token equality join in all cases. If the number of candidates cannot be substantially reduced using the prefix approach, the advantage of the smaller candidate set might be lost due to the overhead of doing the join on the prefixes.

[1]http://dblp.uni-trier.de/xml/
[2]SIGMOD, VLDB/PVLDB, ICDE, PODS, ICDT, TODS, VLDB Journal

6.3   SIZE FILTER

A simple filter that avoids computing the intersection for all pairs is the *size filter* [Arasu et al., 2006, Bayardo et al., 2007], which prunes pairs of sets based on their cardinalities. The size filter is applicable to both overlap and Jaccard constraints:

$$O(X, Y) \geq t \Rightarrow \min(|X|, |Y|) \geq t \tag{6.1}$$
$$J(X, Y) \geq \tau \Rightarrow \tau|X| \leq |Y| \wedge \tau|Y| \leq |X| \tag{6.2}$$

The similarity between two sets is computed only if the size filter condition is met. This condition is checked efficiently and can be combined with all of the techniques discussed in this chapter.

6.4   POSITIONAL FILTER

The *positional filter* [Xiao et al., 2008b] assumes sorted arrays of tokens. Given a token set X, the respective array of tokens is denoted with x. The positional filter is based on the observation that two arrays x and y with a common token w can be pruned depending on the position of the matching token. Using the position filter might allow to prune candidates produced by the prefix filter as shown in the following example [Xiao et al., 2011].

Example 6.4   Consider $x = [a, b, c, d, e]$, $y = [b, c, d, e, f]$ and a Jaccard threshold of $\tau = 0.8$. The prefix of length $k = |x| - t|x| + 1 = |y| - t|y| + 1 = 2$ is underlined:

$$x = [\underline{a, b}, c, d, e]$$
$$y = [\underline{b, c}, d, e, f]$$

The pair (x, y) is in the candidate set of the prefix filter since the prefixes have the token b in common. But the pair is not in the result set since the overlap, $O(x, y) = 4$, does not meet the overlap threshold $t = 5$ that corresponds to the Jaccard threshold $\tau = 0.8$.

We can compute an upper bound on the overlap based on the prefixes and the token lengths, without looking at the tokens to the right of the prefixes. We split the arrays into two parts based on the matching token b, $x_l = [a, b]$, $x_r = [c, d, e]$ and $y_l = [b]$, $y_r = [c, d, e, f]$. Then, due to the sorting, the overlap between x and y can be expressed as $O(x, y) = O(x_l, y_l) + O(x_r, y_r)$. We know $O(x_l, y_l) = 1$, thus $O(x_r, y_r) \geq 4$ is required to reach the threshold $t = 5$. This cannot be reached since $|x_r| < 4$, i.e., there are not enough tokens in x_r. The position filter principle discussed in the example is generalized as follows.

Theorem 6.5   Position Filter Principle.   *[Xiao et al., 2008b] Given arrays x and y with the elements sorted in ascending order according to a strict total order defined on the elements of both arrays, and an integer threshold t. If x and y have a common element $x[i] = y[j]$, then*

$$O(x, y) \geq t \Rightarrow O(x[1..i], y[1..j]) + \min(|x| - i, |y| - j) \geq t \tag{6.3}$$

The position filter is used to stop early during the computation of the intersection. Xiao et al. [2008b] use the position filter together with the prefix filter and leverage the common tokens found during the join of the prefixes. This is possible since the tokens to the right of the prefix need not be accessed.

6.5   PARTITIONING FILTER

The *partitioning filter* [Xiao et al., 2008b] generalizes the size filter (which establishes an upper bound $O(x, y) \leq \min(|x|, |y|)$) and the position filter. The partitioning filter assumes sorted sets of tokens, which are denoted with x and y. The core idea is to partition the arrays x and y into subarrays x_l, x_r and y_l, y_r such that $O(x, y) = O(x_l, y_l) + O(x_r, y_r)$. Then the size filter can be applied to the pair (x_l, y_l) and (x_r, y_r) individually and the resulting lower bound can be tightened by adding up the two lower bounds.

The partitioning is done by picking a position i in array x and splitting x into the left partition $x_l = x[1 \ldots i]$ and the right partition $x_r = x[i + 1 \ldots |x|]$. Array y is split based on the token $x[i]$ into $y_l = y[1 \ldots j]$ and $y_r = y[j + 1 \ldots |y|]$ such that $y[j] \leq x[i]$ and $y[j + 1] > x[i]$. Note that the token $x[i]$ does not need to be present in y.

Since the arrays are sorted and the tokens are unique within each array, all the tokens in x_l and y_l are smaller or equal to $x[i]$ and all the tokens in x_r and y_r are larger than $x[i]$. The overlap between x_l and y_r is zero as is the overlap between x_r and y_l. Thus the overlap between x and y is $O(x, y) = O(x_l, y_l) + O(x_r, y_r)$. We use the size filter for each of the partitions and get the following upper bound:

$$O(x, y) = O(x_l, y_l) + O(x_r, y_r) \leq \min(i, j) + \min(|x| - i, |y| - j) \tag{6.4}$$

This upper bound is at least as tight as the size upper bound on x and y, i.e., $\min(i, j) + \min(|x| - i, |y| - j) \leq \min(|x|, |y|)$. This suggests that the same principle can be recursively applied to the pairs (x_l, y_l) and (x_r, y_r). When x_l is further partitioned into $x[1 \ldots k]$ and $x[k + 1 \ldots i]$, and y_l is partitioned into $y[1 \ldots m]$ and $y[m + 1 \ldots j]$ using token $x[k]$, the new upper bound is $O(x, y) \leq \min(k, m) + \min(i - k, j - m) + \min(|x| - i, |y| - j)$.

6.6   FURTHER READINGS

The token equality join was first applied to q-grams on strings by Gravano et al. [2001], where the overlap between the q-grams is used as a filter for the string edit distance, called *count filter*. Augsten et al. [2008] apply the token equality join for similarity joins between trees using *pq*-grams.

The prefix filter for token similarity joins was introduced by Chaudhuri et al. [2006] for relational database systems. A principle similar to the prefix filter was introduced earlier by Sarawagi and Kirpal [2004] in the OptMerge algorithm. OptMerge is a main memory algorithm based on an inverted list index, in which for each token a sorted list of token set IDs is stored. The overlap between a given token set X and the indexed sets is computed by merging the ID-lists for all tokens in X and counting for each ID the number of its appearances in the lists. All IDs that appear in at least t lists satisfy the overlap constraint for the threshold t. To improve the efficiency of merging ID-lists, the OptMerge algorithm sorts all ID-lists by their length. The $t - 1$ longest lists are considered only for set IDs that appear at least once in the remaining (shorter) lists, thus avoiding to merge the long lists. The sorting criterion of tokens (the list length) corresponds to the document frequency of a token, i.e., the number of token sets in which it appears.

In terms of prefixes, the OptMerge approach is equivalent to prefixes that consist of the tokens of X minus the $t - 1$ largest tokens among all token sets. This leads to larger prefixes compared to the prefix approach presented in Section 6.2, where the prefix of X consists of all tokens except the $t - 1$ largest tokens of X, also if they are not within the $t - 1$ largest tokens globally.

Main memory algorithms based on inverted list indexes like OptMerge were also proposed by Bayardo et al. [2007] (AllPairs) and Xiao et al. [2008b] (ppjoin/ppjoin+). Wang et al. [2012b] present adaptive, variable length prefixes. Ribeiro and Härder [2011] introduce the concept of min-prefixes, which allows them to dynamically maintain the length of the inverted list and reduce the cost for the candidate generation. Xiao et al. [2008b] use the partitioning filter principle together with the prefix filter in their main memory algorithm for similarity joins. When the first matching token in the prefixes of x and y is found, the partitioning filter is applied to the remaining tokens in x and y and is called *suffix filter*. Xiao et al. [2011] show the implementation of prefix filter, size filter, and positional filter as SQL queries. The PartEnum algorithm by Arasu et al. [2006] is based on the pigeon hole principle. The ordered token sets are partitioned and hashed to signatures, which are used to produce candidate sets.

All techniques discussed so far compute the exact set similarity join. An approximate technique based on LSH (Locality Sensitive Hashing) was presented by Gionis et al. [1999]. Broder et al. [1997] use min-wise independent permutations to approximate the set similarity join.

Mazeika et al. [2007] present the VSol estimator for estimating the selectivity of approximate string queries based on an inverted q-gram index. The time to estimate the selectivity is independent of the number of database strings and linear w.r.t. the length of the query string. Lee et al. [2009] estimate the selectivity of set similarity joins using Min-Hash signatures.

CHAPTER 7

Conclusion

In this book we have described the basic concepts and techniques to compute similarity joins in relational databases. Similarity joins are particularly relevant for complex objects, including string and trees, where equality frequently yields unsatisfactory results.

Edit-based similarities quantify the difference between two objects by the number of basic edit operations that are required to transform one object into another. The smaller the number of required edit operations, the more similar the objects are. Edit-based distances are popular across a large number of applications since edit distances are intuitive, guarantee the minimal sequence of edit operations, and can be tailored to different applications by adapting the cost model.

The main challenge with edit distances is their high computational cost. A frequent approach to ameliorate the costs of computing the edit distance are filters. A filter discards unpromising tuples before evaluating the similarity predicate. The evaluation of the filter is much faster than the evaluation of the similarity predicate, which boosts the overall performance.

Various filters have been proposed for edit-based distances. Our main focus are token-based filters. Token-based filters represent objects by sets (or bags) of tokens and express the similarity between objects using set operations like intersection. This makes token-based filters very appealing for relational database systems, which are geared to sets and multisets. Token-based filters have been developed for many data types, including strings, trees, and graphs. Examples of tokens are the words of a document, substrings of fixed length of a string (called q-grams), or subtrees of a fixed shape of a tree (called pq-grams). Tokens are used to assess the similarity of two objects. Intuitively, two objects are similar if they share many tokens. For example, two text documents are considered similar if they have many words in common.

To further reduce the costs of similarity computations, filter and refine approaches have been developed. The goal of the filter step is to cheaply identify candidate pairs for which the exact similarity must be computed. Non-candidate pairs do not have to be considered because their similarity is not sufficient to be included in the result. We describe various filter techniques, and provide lower and upper bounds that can be used to efficiently compute similarity joins.

Bibliography

Tatsuya Akutsu, Daiji Fukagawa, Atsuhiro Takasu, and Takeyuki Tamura. Exact algorithms for computing the tree edit distance between unordered trees. *Theor. Comp. Sci.*, 412(4-5):352–364, 2011. DOI: 10.1016/j.tcs.2010.10.002. 22

Tatsuya Akutsu, Takeyuki Tamura, Daiji Fukagawa, and Atsuhiro Takasu. Efficient exponential time algorithms for edit distance between unordered trees. In *Combinatorial Pattern Matching*, pages 360–372. 2012. DOI: 10.1007/978-3-642-31265-6_29. 22

Tatsuya Akutsu, Daiji Fukagawa, Magnús M. Halldórsson, Atsuhiro Takasu, and Keisuke Tanaka. Approximation and parameterized algorithms for common subtrees and edit distance between unordered trees. *Theor. Comp. Sci.*, 470:10–22, 2013. DOI: 10.1016/j.tcs.2012.11.017. 22

Shurug Al-Khalifa, H. V. Jagadish, Jignesh M. Patel, Yuqing Wu, Nick Koudas, and Divesh Srivastava. Structural joins: A primitive for efficient XML query pattern matching. In *Proc. 18th Int. Conf. on Data Engineering*, pages 141–152, 2002. DOI: 10.1109/ICDE.2002.994704. 39

Kiyoko F. Aoki, Atsuko Yamaguchi, Y. Okuno, Tatsuya Akutsu, Nobuhisa Ueda, Minoru Kanehisa, and Hiroshi Mamitsuka. Efficient tree-matching methods for accurate carbohydrate database queries. *Genome Informatics*, 14:134–143, 2003. 3

Alberto Apostolico and Zvi Galil. The longest common subsequence problem revisited. *Algorithmica*, 2(1):315–336, 1987. DOI: 10.1007/BF01840365. 22

Arvind Arasu, Venkatesh Ganti, and Raghav Kaushik. Efficient exact set-similarity joins. In *Proc. 32nd Int. Conf. on Very Large Data Bases*, pages 918–929, 2006. 78, 87, 89

Nikolaus Augsten, Michael H. Böhlen, and Johann Gamper. Reducing the integration of public administration databases to approximate tree matching. In *Electronic Government – Third International Conference*, pages 102–107, 2004. DOI: 10.1007/978-3-540-30078-6_17. 2

Nikolaus Augsten, Michael H. Böhlen, and Johann Gamper. Approximate matching of hierarchical data using *pq*-grams. In *Proc. 31st Int. Conf. on Very Large Data Bases*, pages 301–312, 2005. 6, 30, 58

Nikolaus Augsten, Michael H. Böhlen, and Johann Gamper. An incrementally maintainable index for approximate lookups in hierarchical data. In *Proc. 32nd Int. Conf. on Very Large Data Bases*, pages 247–258, 2006. 37

Nikolaus Augsten, Michael H. Böhlen, Curtis Dyreson, and Johann Gamper. Approximate joins for data-centric XML. In *Proc. 24th Int. Conf. on Data Engineering*, pages 814–823, 2008. DOI: 10.1109/ICDE.2008.4497490. 43, 58, 88

Nikolaus Augsten, Denilson Barbosa, Michael H. Böhlen, and Themis Palpanas. TASM: Top-k approximate subtree matching. In *Proc. 26th Int. Conf. on Data Engineering*, pages 353–364, 2010a. DOI: 10.1109/ICDE.2010.5447905. 23

Nikolaus Augsten, Michael H. Böhlen, and Johann Gamper. The *pq*-gram distance between ordered labeled trees. *ACM Trans. Database Syst.*, 35(1):1–36, 2010b. 36, 58, 72

Roberto J. Bayardo, Yiming Ma, and Ramakrishnan Srikant. Scaling up all pairs similarity search. In *Proc. 16th Int. World Wide Web Conf.*, 2007. DOI: 10.1145/1242572.1242591. 87, 89

Philip Bille. A survey on tree edit distance and related problems. *Theoretical Computer Science*, 337(1-3):217–239, 2005. DOI: 10.1016/j.tcs.2004.12.030. 23

Guillaume Blin, Alain Denise, Serge Dulucq, Claire Herrbach, and Hélène Touzet. Alignments of RNA structures. *IEEE/ACM Transactions on Computational Biology and Bioinformatics*, 7 (2):309–322, 2010. DOI: 10.1109/TCBB.2008.28. 3

Andrei Z. Broder, Steven C. Glassman, Mark S. Manasse, and Geoffrey Zweig. Syntactic clustering of the web. *Computer Networks*, 29(8-13):1157–1166, 1997. DOI: 10.1016/S0169-7552(97)00031-7. 89

David Buttler. A short survey of document structure similarity algorithms. In *Proceedings of the International Conference on Internet Computing*, pages 3–9, 2004. 30, 58

Joe Celko. Trees, databases and SQL. *Database Programming & Design*, 7(10):48–57, 1994. 39

Joe Celko. *Trees and Hierarchies in SQL for Smarties*. Morgan Kaufmann Publishers Inc., 2004. 39

Surajit Chaudhuri and Raghav Kaushik. Extending autocompletion to tolerate errors. In *Proc. ACM SIGMOD Int. Conf. on Management of Data*, pages 707–718, 2009. DOI: 10.1145/1559845.1559919. 78

Surajit Chaudhuri, Venkatesh Ganti, and Raghav Kaushik. A primitive operator for similarity joins in data cleaning. In *Proc. 22nd Int. Conf. on Data Engineering*, 2006. DOI: 10.1109/ICDE.2006.9. 83, 84, 88

Paolo Ciaccia, Marco Patella, and Pavel Zezula. M-tree: An efficient access method for similarity search in metric spaces. In *Proc. 23th Int. Conf. on Very Large Data Bases*, pages 426–435, 1997. 78

David DeHaan, David Toman, Mariano P. Consens, and M. Tamer Özsu. A comprehensive XQuery to SQL translation using dynamic interval encoding. In *Proc. ACM SIGMOD Int. Conf. on Management of Data*, pages 623–634, 2003. DOI: 10.1145/872757.872832. 39

Erik D. Demaine, Shay Mozes, Benjamin Rossman, and Oren Weimann. An optimal decomposition algorithm for tree edit distance. In *34th Int. Colloquium on Automata, Languages, and Programming*, pages 146–157, 2007. DOI: 10.1007/978-3-540-73420-8_15. 18

Lee R. Dice. Measures of the amount of ecologic association between species. *Ecology*, 26(3): 297–302, 1945. DOI: 10.2307/1932409. 27

Serge Dulucq and Hélène Touzet. Analysis of tree edit distance algorithms. In *Combinatorial Pattern Matching (CPM 2003)*, pages 83–95. Springer, 2003. DOI: 10.1007/3-540-44888-8_7. 18

Dandy Fenz, Dustin Lange, Astrid Rheinländer, Felix Naumann, and Ulf Leser. Efficient similarity search in very large string sets. In *Proc. 24th Int. Conf. on Scientific and Statistical Database Management*, pages 262–279, 2012. DOI: 10.1007/978-3-642-31235-9_18. 78

Jan Finis, Martin Raiber, Nikolaus Augsten, Robert Brunel, Alfons Kemper, and Franz Färber. RWS-Diff: Flexible and efficient change detection in hierarchical data. In *Proc. 22nd ACM Int. Conf. on Information and Knowledge Management*, 2013. 23

Xinbo Gao, Bing Xiao, Dacheng Tao, and Xuelong Li. A survey of graph edit distance. *Pattern Analysis and Applications*, 13(1):113–129, 2010. DOI: 10.1007/s10044-008-0141-y. 23

Minos Garofalakis and Amit Kumar. Correlating XML data streams using tree-edit distance embeddings. In *Proc. 22nd ACM SIGACT-SIGMOD-SIGART Symp. on Principles of Database Systems*, pages 143–154, 2003. DOI: 10.1145/773153.773168. 31

Minos Garofalakis and Amit Kumar. XML stream processing using tree-edit distance embeddings. *ACM Transactions on Database Systems*, 30(1):279–332, 2005. DOI: 10.1145/1061318.1061326. 58

Aristides Gionis, Piotr Indyk, and Rajeev Motwani. Similarity search in high dimensions via hashing. In *Proc. 25th Int. Conf. on Very Large Data Bases*, pages 518–529, 1999. 89

Luis Gravano, Panagiotis G. Ipeirotis, H. V. Jagadish, Nick Koudas, S. Muthukrishnan, and Divesh Srivastava. Approximate string joins in a database (almost) for free. In *Proc. 27th Int. Conf. on Very Large Data Bases*, pages 491–500, 2001. 64, 65, 66, 78, 88

96 BIBLIOGRAPHY

Luis Gravano, Panagiotis G. Ipeirotis, H. V. Jagadish, Nick Koudas, S. Muthukrishnan, and Divesh Srivastava. Approximate string joins in a database (almost) for free — Erratum. Technical Report CUCS-011-03, Department of Computer Science, Columbia University, 2003. 67

Torsten Grust. Accelerating XPath location steps. In *Proc. ACM SIGMOD Int. Conf. on Management of Data*, pages 109–120, 2002. DOI: 10.1145/564691.564705. 39

Sudipto Guha, H. V. Jagadish, Nick Koudas, Divesh Srivastava, and Ting Yu. Approximate XML joins. In *Proc. ACM SIGMOD Int. Conf. on Management of Data*, pages 287–298, 2002. DOI: 10.1145/564691.564725. 18, 70, 76, 78

Marios Hadjieleftheriou and Divesh Srivastava. Approximate string processing. *Foundations and Trends in Databases*, 2(4):267–402, 2011. DOI: 10.1561/1900000010. 78

Richard W. Hamming. Error detecting and error correcting codes. *Bell System Technical Journal*, 26(2):147–160, 1950. DOI: 10.1002/j.1538-7305.1950.tb00463.x. 22

Shoichi Higuchi, Tomohiro Kan, Yoshiyuki Yamamoto, and Kouichi Hirata. An A* algorithm for computing edit distance between rooted labeled unordered trees. In *JSAI-isAI Workshops*, pages 186–196, 2011. DOI: 10.1007/978-3-642-32090-3_17. 22

Yair Horesh, Ramit Mehr, and Ron Unger. Designing an A* algorithm for calculating edit distance between rooted-unordered trees. *J. Computational Biology*, 13(6):1165–1176, 2006. DOI: 10.1089/cmb.2006.13.1165. 22

Paul Jaccard. Distribution de la flore alpine dans le bassin des dranses et dans quelques régions voisines. *Bulletin de la Société Vaudoise des Sciences Naturelles*, 37:241–272, 1901. 26

Shengyue Ji, Guoliang Li, Chen Li, and Jianhua Feng. Efficient interactive fuzzy keyword search. In *Proc. 18th Int. World Wide Web Conf.*, pages 371–380, 2009. DOI: 10.1145/1526709.1526760. 78

Tao Jiang, Lusheng Wang, and Kaizhong Zhang. Alignment of trees—an alternative to tree edit. *Theoretical Computer Science*, 143(1):137–148, 1995. DOI: 10.1016/0304-3975(95)80015-8. 23

Karin Kailing, Hans-Peter Kriegel, Stefan Schönauer, and Thomas Seidl. Efficient similarity search for hierarchical data in large databases. In *Advances in Database Technology, Proc. 9th Int. Conf. on Extending Database Technology*, pages 676–693, 2004. DOI: 10.1007/978-3-540-24741-8_39. 70

Richard M. Karp and Michael O. Rabin. Efficient randomized pattern-matching algorithms. *IBM J. Res. Dev.*, 31(2):249–260, 1987. DOI: 10.1147/rd.312.0249. 56

Philip N. Klein. Computing the edit-distance between unrooted ordered trees. In *Proc. 6th Annual European Symp. on Algorithms*, pages 91–102, 1998. DOI: 10.1007/3-540-68530-8_8. 18

Hongrae Lee, Raymond T. Ng, and Kyuseok Shim. Power-law based estimation of set similarity join size. *Proc. VLDB Endow.*, 2:658–669, 2009. 89

Vladimir I. Levenshtein. Binary codes capable of correcting spurious insertions and deletions of ones. *Problems of Information Transmission*, 1:8–17, 1965. 11

Chen Li, Bin Wang, and Xiaochun Yang. VGRAM: Improving performance of approximate queries on string collections using variable-length grams. In *Proc. 33rd Int. Conf. on Very Large Data Bases*, pages 303–314, 2007. 6, 59, 78

Chen Li, Jiaheng Lu, and Yiming Lu. Efficient merging and filtering algorithms for approximate string searches. In *Proc. 24th Int. Conf. on Data Engineering*, pages 257–266, 2008. DOI: 10.1109/ICDE.2008.4497434. 78

Guoliang Li, Shengyue Ji, Chen Li, and Jianhua Feng. Efficient type-ahead search on relational data: a TASTIER approach. In *Proc. ACM SIGMOD Int. Conf. on Management of Data*, pages 695–706, 2009. DOI: 10.1145/1559845.1559918. 78

Guoliang Li, Dong Deng, Jiannan Wang, and Jianhua Feng. Pass-join: a partition-based method for similarity joins. *Proc. VLDB Endowment*, 5(3):253–264, 2011. 78

Arturas Mazeika, Michael H. Böhlen, Nick Koudas, and Divesh Srivastava. Estimating the selectivity of approximate string queries. *ACM Trans. Database Syst.*, 32, 2007. DOI: 10.1145/1242524.1242529. 89

Saul B. Needleman and Christian D. Wunsch. A general method applicable to the search for similarities in the amino acid sequence of two proteins. *Journal of Molecular Biology*, 48:443–453, 1970. DOI: 10.1016/0022-2836(70)90057-4. 22

Patrick O'Neil, Elizabeth O'Neil, Shankar Pal, Istvan Cseri, Gideon Schaller, and Nigel Westbury. ORDPATHs: Insert-friendly XML node labels. In *Proc. ACM SIGMOD Int. Conf. on Management of Data*, pages 903–908, 2004. DOI: 10.1145/1007568.1007686. 39

Mateusz Pawlik and Nikolaus Augsten. RTED: A robust algorithm for the tree edit distance. *Proc. VLDB Endowment*, 5(4):334–345, 2011. 18

Jianbin Qin, Wei Wang, Yifei Lu, Chuan Xiao, and Xuemin Lin. Efficient exact edit similarity query processing with the asymmetric signature scheme. In *Proc. ACM SIGMOD Int. Conf. on Management of Data*, pages 1033–1044, 2011. DOI: 10.1145/1989323.1989431. 78

Leonardo A. Ribeiro and Theo Härder. Generalizing prefix filtering to improve set similarity joins. *Inf. Syst.*, 36(1):62–78, 2011. DOI: 10.1016/j.is.2010.07.003. 89

Hanan Samet. *Foundations of Multidimensional and Metric Data Structures*. Morgan Kaufmann Publishers Inc., 2005. 78

Alberto Sanfeliu and King-Sun Fu. A distance measure between attributed relational graphs for pattern recognition. *IEEE Trans. Systems, Man, and Cybernetics*, 13(3):353–362, 1983. DOI: 10.1109/TSMC.1983.6313167. 23

Sunita Sarawagi and Alok Kirpal. Efficient set joins on similarity predicates. In *Proc. ACM SIGMOD Int. Conf. on Management of Data*, pages 743–754, 2004. DOI: 10.1145/1007568.1007652. 88

Stanley M. Selkow. The tree-to-tree editing problem. *Inf. Proc. Letters*, 6(6):184–186, 1977. DOI: 10.1016/0020-0190(77)90064-3. 23

Dennis Shasha, Jason Tsong-Li Wang, Kaizhong Zhang, and Frank Y. Shih. Exact and approximate algorithms for unordered tree matching. *IEEE Trans. Systems, Man, and Cybernetics*, 24 (4):668–678, 1994. DOI: 10.1109/21.286387. 22

Yasin N. Silva, Walid G. Aref, Per-Åke Larson, Spencer Pearson, and Mohamed H. Ali. Similarity queries: their conceptual evaluation, transformations, and processing. *VLDB J.*, 22(3): 395–420, 2013a. DOI: 10.1007/s00778-012-0296-4. 78

Yasin N. Silva, Spencer Pearson, and Jason A. Cheney. Database similarity join for metric spaces. In *Proc. 6th Int. Conf. on Similarity Search and Applications*, pages 266–279, 2013b. DOI: 10.1145/1366102.1366104. 78

Volker Springel, Simon D. M. White, Adrian Jenkins, Carlos S. Frenk, Naoki Yoshida, Liang Gao, Julio Navarro, Robert Thacker, Darren Croton, John Helly, John A. Peacock, Shaun Cole, Peter Thomas, Hugh Couchman, August Evrard, Jörg Colberg, and Frazer Pearce. Simulations of the formation, evolution and clustering of galaxies and quasars. *Nature*, 435, 2005. DOI: 10.1038/nature03597. 4

Erkki Sutinen and Jorma Tarhio. On using q-gram locations in approximate string matching. In *Proc. 3rd Annual European Symp. on Algorithms*, pages 327–340, 1995. DOI: 10.1007/3-540-60313-1_153. 65

Erkki Sutinen and Jorma Tarhio. Filtration with q-samples in approximate string matching. In *Proceedings of the 7th Annual Symposium on Combinatorial Pattern Matching*, pages 50–63, 1996. DOI: 10.1007/3-540-61258-0_4. 64

Igor Tatarinov, Stratis Viglas, Kevin S. Beyer, Jayavel Shanmugasundaram, Eugene J. Shekita, and Chun Zhang. Storing and querying ordered XML using a relational database system. In *Proc. ACM SIGMOD Int. Conf. on Management of Data*, pages 204–215, 2002. DOI: 10.1145/564691.564715. 39

Shirish Tatikonda and Srinivasan Parthasarathy. Hashing tree-structured data: Methods and applications. In *Proc. 26th Int. Conf. on Data Engineering*, pages 429–440, 2010. DOI: 10.1109/ICDE.2010.5447882. 42, 58, 59

Esko Ukkonen. Approximate string-matching with q-grams and maximal matches. *Theor. Comp. Sci.*, 92(1):191–211, 1992. DOI: 10.1016/0304-3975(92)90143-4. 6, 29

Gabriel Valiente. An efficient bottom-up distance between trees. In *Proc. 8th Int. Symp. String Processing and Information Retrieval*, pages 212–219, 2001. DOI: 10.1109/SPIRE.2001.989761. 23

Guoren Wang, Bin Wang, Xiaochun Yang, and Ge Yu. Efficiently indexing large sparse graphs for similarity search. *IEEE Trans. Knowl. and Data Eng.*, 24(3):440–451, 2012a. DOI: 10.1109/TKDE.2010.28. 23, 59

Jiannan Wang, Jianhua Feng, and Guoliang Li. Trie-join: efficient trie-based string similarity joins with edit-distance constraints. *Proc. VLDB Endowment*, 3(1-2):1219–1230, 2010. 78

Jiannan Wang, Guoliang Li, and Jianhua Fe. Fast-join: An efficient method for fuzzy token matching based string similarity join. In *Proc. 27th Int. Conf. on Data Engineering*, pages 458–469, 2011. DOI: 10.1109/ICDE.2011.5767865. 78

Jiannan Wang, Guoliang Li, and Jianhua Feng. Can we beat the prefix filtering? An adaptive framework for similarity join and search. In *Proc. ACM SIGMOD Int. Conf. on Management of Data*, pages 85–96, 2012b. DOI: 10.1145/2213836.2213847. 89

Wei Wang, Chuan Xiao, Xuemin Lin, and Chengqi Zhang. Efficient approximate entity extraction with edit distance constraints. In *Proc. ACM SIGMOD Int. Conf. on Management of Data*, pages 759–770, 2009. DOI: 10.1145/1559845.1559925. 78

Xiaoli Wang, Xiaofeng Ding, Anthony K. H. Tung, Shanshan Ying, and Hai Jin. An efficient graph indexing method. In *Proc. 28th Int. Conf. on Data Engineering*, pages 210–221, 2012c. DOI: 10.1109/ICDE.2012.28. 23

William E. Winkler. String comparator metrics and enhanced decision rules in the fellegi-sunter model of record linkage. In *Proceedings of the Section on Survey Research*, pages 354–359, 1990. 22

Chuan Xiao, Wei Wang, and Xuemin Lin. Ed-Join: An efficient algorithm for similarity joins with edit distance constraints. In *Proc. 34th Int. Conf. on Very Large Data Bases*, 2008a. 78

Chuan Xiao, Wei Wang, Xuemin Lin, and Jeffrey Xu Yu. Efficient similarity joins for near duplicate detection. In *Proc. 17th Int. World Wide Web Conf.*, 2008b. DOI: 10.1145/1367497.1367516. 84, 87, 88, 89

Chuan Xiao, Wei Wang, Xuemin Lin, Jeffrey Xu Yu, and Guoren Wang. Efficient similarity joins for near-duplicate detection. *ACM Trans. Database Syst.*, 36(3):15:1–15:41, 2011. DOI: 10.1145/2000824.2000825. 85, 86, 87, 89

Rui Yang, Panos Kalnis, and Anthony K. H. Tung. Similarity evaluation on tree-structured data. In *Proc. ACM SIGMOD Int. Conf. on Management of Data*, pages 754–765, 2005. DOI: 10.1145/1066157.1066243. 30, 58, 74, 76

Wuu Yang. Identifying syntactic differences between two programs. *Software — Practice & Experience*, 21(7):739–755, 1991. DOI: 10.1002/spe.4380210706. 23

Xiaochun Yang, Bin Wang, and Chen Li. Cost-based variable-length-gram selection for string collections to support approximate queries efficiently. In *Proc. ACM SIGMOD Int. Conf. on Management of Data*, pages 353–364, 2008. DOI: 10.1145/1376616.1376655. 59, 78

Zhiping Zeng, Anthony K. H. Tung, Jianyong Wang, Jianhua Feng, and Lizhu Zhou. Comparing stars: On approximating graph edit distance. *Proc. VLDB Endowment*, 2(1):25–36, 2009. 23, 59

Pavel Zezula, Giuseppe Amato, Vlastislav Dohnal, and Michal Batko. *Similarity Search—The Metric Space Approach*, volume 32 of *Advances in Database Systems*. Springer, 2006. 35, 49, 78

Chun Zhang, Jeffrey F. Naughton, David J. DeWitt, Qiong Luo, and Guy M. Lohman. On supporting containment queries in relational database management systems. In *Proc. ACM SIGMOD Int. Conf. on Management of Data*, pages 425–436, 2001. DOI: 10.1145/376284.375722. 39

Kaizhong Zhang. Algorithms for the constrained editing distance between ordered labeled trees and related problems. *Pattern Recognition*, 28(3):463–474, 1995. DOI: 10.1016/0031-3203(94)00109-Y. 18, 76

Kaizhong Zhang and Tao Jiang. Some max snp-hard results concerning unordered labeled trees. *Inf. Proc. Letters*, 49(5):249–254, 1994. DOI: 10.1016/0020-0190(94)90062-0. 21

Kaizhong Zhang and Dennis Shasha. Simple fast algorithms for the editing distance between trees and related problems. *SIAM J. on Comput.*, 18(6), 1989. DOI: 10.1137/0218082. 18, 58

Kaizhong Zhang, Richard Statman, and Dennis Shasha. On the editing distance between unordered labeled trees. *Inf. Proc. Letters*, 42(3):133–139, 1992. DOI: 10.1016/0020-0190(92)90136-J. 8, 19, 21

Zhenjie Zhang, Marios Hadjieleftheriou, Beng Chin Ooi, and Divesh Srivastava.   Bed-tree: an all-purpose index structure for string similarity search based on edit distance. In *Proc. ACM SIGMOD Int. Conf. on Management of Data*, pages 915–926, 2010. DOI: 10.1145/1807167.1807266. 78

Xiang Zhao, Chuan Xiao, Xuemin Lin, and Wei Wang. Efficient graph similarity joins with edit distance constraints. In *Proc. 28th Int. Conf. on Data Engineering*, pages 834–845, 2012. DOI: 10.1109/ICDE.2012.91. 6, 23, 59

Authors' Biographies

NIKOLAUS AUGSTEN

Nikolaus Augsten is a professor in the Department of Computer Science at the University of Salzburg, Austria, where he heads the Database Group. He received his Ph.D. degree in computer science from Aalborg University, Denmark, in 2008, and holds a M.Sc. degree from Graz University of Technology, Austria. Prior to joining the University of Salzburg in 2013, he was an assistant professor at the Free University of Bolzano, Italy. He was on leave at TU München, Germany, in 2010/2011 and visited Washington State University for six months in 2005/2006. His main research interests include similarity search queries over massive data collections, approximate matching techniques for complex data structures, efficient index structures for distance computations, and top-k queries. For his work on top-k approximate subtree matching he received the Best Paper Award at the IEEE International Conference on Data Engineering in 2010. Currently, he serves as an Associate Editor for the *VLDB Journal*.

MICHAEL H. BÖHLEN

Michael H. Böhlen is a professor of computer science at the University of Zürich where he heads the Database Technology Group. His research interests include various aspects of data management, and have focused on time-varying information, data warehousing and data analysis, and similarity search. He received his M.Sc. and Ph.D. degrees from ETH Zürich in 1990 and 1994, respectively. Before joining the University of Zürich he visited the University of Arizona for one year, and was a faculty member at Aalborg University for eight years and the Free University of Bozen-Bolzano for six years. He was program co-chair of the 39th International Conference on Very Large Data Bases and served as an Associate Editor for the *VLDB Journal.* He served as a PC member for SIGMOD, VLDB, ICDE, and EDBT. Currently, he serves as an Associate Editor for ACM TODS, and he is a member of the VLDB Endowment's Board of Trustees.

Index

Printed in the United States
by Baker & Taylor Publisher Services